West Academic Publishing's Law School Advisory Board

Bitcoin, Blockchain, and Crypto

Del Wright Jr.
Professor
University of Missouri-Kansas City Law School

A SHORT & HAPPY GUIDE® SERIES

WEST
ACADEMIC
PUBLISHING

© 2020 LEG, Inc. d/b/a West Academic

444 Cedar Street, Suite 700
St. Paul, MN 55101
1-877-888-1330

Printed in the United States of America

ISBN: 978-1-68467-226-4

Preface

Why do we need crypto?

For readers looking for an answer to that question, the best answer I have found is the essay, *A World Without Bitcoin*, by Alex Gladstein, Chief Strategy Officer at the Human Rights Foundation. That essay is available on the February 11, 2020 Unchained podcast, hosted by Laura Shin, available and transcribed at www.unchained podcast.com/alex-gladstein-on-a-world-without-bitcoin/.

This book is not written to answer that question. Instead, it aims to give the reader three things:

1) an overview of blockchains: how they work, how they are controlled, as well as the technological and policy challenges facing them;

2) an explanation of the value proposition for blockchain technologies and cryptoassets (crypto); and

3) an analysis of the laws that apply to crypto.

Although there is a lot of hype surrounding blockchains, many technologies are still in their infancy. Nevertheless, because blockchains serve as trust machines that can limit the need for, and costs of, third-party intermediaries, the possible uses of the technology are limitless. Thus, it is important for entrepreneurs, lawyers, policy makers, and regulators to understand the technology and its applications. This book provides an on-ramp.

> *Better a diamond with a flaw than a pebble without.*
> —Confucius

This is a fast-moving technological and legal area, and the goal of this book is to provide an introduction and overview. To that end, in attempting to explain largely technical areas in an understandable way, it was often necessary to simplify concepts to make them accessible to readers. That created a challenge in drawing the line between too simple and too detailed. As with most things in life, "the perfect is the enemy of the good," and I hope this book strikes the right balance.

Del Wright Jr.

12 April 2020

Acknowledgments

First and foremost, I would like to thank Cheryl for serving as lead editor, logic critiquer, task enforcer, and chief motivator. As with most of my accomplishments, I could not have done this without you.

Next, I would like to thank Nancy for setting all of this in motion, and Brandon, who began this journey with the question, "Prof. Wright, what do you know about bitcoin?" I would also like to thank Louis and Megan at West Academic, for entrusting me with this project and providing the support to bring it home.

I would also like to thank all the people who supported this project, either knowingly or unknowingly, through their work. That last group includes, but is not limited to, the following, with my sincere apologies for all omissions:

The Students

Ryan, Jazmine, Austin, Dan, Fluffy, Nihit, Sarah, Vince, Dara, Devin, Madeline, Kristen, Nate, Megan, Iman, and Tony

My Academic Colleagues

Andrew Hinkes, Carla Reyes, Dean Tonya Evans, Jonathan Glater, Stephen Wilkes, Kenneth Ferguson, Jamila Jefferson Jones, Khaled Beydoun, Dean Barbara Glesner Fines, Anthony Luppino, Chris Hoyt, and Andre Smith

Crypto & Other Professionals

Matthew Beck and Marissa Arnold at Grayscale Investments, Ilya Tabakh, Jesus A. Rodriguez, Caitlin Long, Andrea Tinianow, Caty Tedman at Cryptokitties, Marty Bent and Matt Odell from *Tales from the Crypt*, Laura Shin from *Unconfirmed* and *Unchained*, Anthony Pompliano at Morgan Creek Digital, David Kintu, Shekhar Gupta at the Government Blockchain Association, Tedrick Housh and Dale

Werts at Lathrop Gage, and Shaun Stallworth at the Jackson County Bar Association

Academic & Professional Institutions

UMKC Law School and Law Review, the John Mercer Langston Writing Workshop, the Southeastern Association of Law Schools (SEALS), the University of Arkansas Bowen School of Law and Law Review, the Harvard Kennedy School, the Harvard Law School Forum on Corporate Governance, and the Practicing Law Institute

Lastly, a special thanks to Prof. Noel Myricks for pushing me, Prof. Richard Boldt for showing me the way, as well as Bibi, Chaun, and the Dels, for setting the bar high.

> *On to the next one.*
> —Jay Z

About the Author

My interest in this subject predates blockchains, and strangely enough, began with a question I asked myself when watching Star Trek: "What do they use for money?" Until bitcoin, I had no satisfactory answer.

In the Star Trek universe, "money" as we know it largely did not exist, mostly because there was a device called a "replicator" that could reproduce almost any non-living thing, including money. Despite the existence of the replicator, people in the Star Trek universe still needed services (haircuts, guitar lessons, etc.), which meant there had to be a way to motivate people to provide those services. The Star Trek Wiki answer is Latinum,

> *"a rare silver liquid used as currency by many worlds, most notably the Ferengi Alliance. Latinum cannot be replicated and the reasons for its rarity are unknown."*

To me, that seemed like something the writers made up to explain what would otherwise be a logical gap in the show.

Then I learned about bitcoin—a non-reproducible digital asset that serves as a store of value, medium of exchange, and unit of account. Bitcoin became, and remains, the most robust answer to the question of what an advanced society would use for money.

With the advent of more-advanced 3D printers and quantum computers, replicators may soon become reality. In fact, Mattershift, a technology startup with alumni from MIT and Yale, are reportedly working on replicator-type 3D printing technology using carbon nanotube membranes. Whether, and when, such technology is viable is anyone's guess. However, one of the likely first uses of such a technology might be to replicate items that serve as stores of value, such as gold, diamonds, or cash.

Those realities piqued my interest in bitcoin and blockchain technologies, as did my educational and professional experiences. I earned a master's degree in public policy from Harvard's Kennedy School, with a focus on financial policy, and a law degree from the University of Chicago. The path I took to get those degrees, however, was anything but traditional.

I left law school after my first year because I realized something was missing in my education. During that first year, we often had to tackle legal issues that were, at their core, financial and economic policy issues, areas I ignored as an undergraduate.

Fortunately, one of my law school professors advised and encouraged me to take the risk of leaving law school to fill the gaps (thanks Prof. Boldt). His advice was spot on: the finance policy program at the Kennedy School was exactly what I needed (fortunately, math was not one of the undergrad areas I ignored). I finished law school at the University of Chicago because it focused on the economic analysis of the law, and embarked on a career that involved finance, law, public policy, and the intersection of all three: tax.

During that career, I structured derivatives (before they exacerbated the financial crisis), advised clients as a business, tax and banking lawyer, represented my country at the US Department of Justice as white-collar prosecutor (pursuing rich people who stole from poor people), and over the last decade, served as a law professor. However, it was not until I discovered bitcoin and blockchain that it all came together: finance, economics, law, public policy and game theory, wrapped neatly in one package—crypto.

Table of Contents

A Short & Happy Guide
to
Bitcoin, Blockchain, and Crypto

PART I

Blockchain Technology

Blockchain Innovation

The innovation of blockchain technologies is that they reduce or eliminate the need for trust and trusted intermediaries in economic relationships. Blockchains are, at their core, trust machines. In a world increasingly both more and less connected, that innovation is valuable, as evidenced by the media attention and investments in blockchain technologies. This book digs deeper into how blockchains serve as trust machines, exploring how blockchain technologies increase the efficiency of trust, explaining some use cases for blockchains, and describing the state of the law for blockchain applications.

From a technical perspective, blockchains are digital ledgers, maintained on a network of computers that keeps an honest, permanent record of unique information ("digital information") owned by one party, and prevent that digital information from being copied or used by anyone other than the owner. When transactions occur over a certain limited period, those transactions are grouped together and recorded into blocks. Those blocks are then added to the ledger of all earlier blocks, forming a blockchain.

One important feature of many blockchains is they are, for the most part, immutable. Once data has been entered into a block and recorded on the blockchain, no one can alter that data. And when a new block is added to a blockchain, it must be consistent with *all* previous blocks. In simple terms, that means that if a user has 10 bitcoins (in general, *B*itcoin relates to the network, and *b*itcoin or "BTC" relates to the crypto) recorded on the blockchain:

1) no one can manipulate the number of bitcoins the user has, and

2) the system would prevent the user from spending more than 10 bitcoins because such a transaction would be inconsistent with all the previous blocks.

In addition, by tracing back the user's transactions it would be possible to see each and every transaction to determine exactly how the user amassed the 10 bitcoins. Immutability allows users to enter into transactions and be assured that counterparties can perform their transactional obligations.

Throughout this book, examples will be used to explain and simplify the mechanics of blockchain transactions. In many of those examples, "Bibi" will serve as one party, often a buyer, and "Chaun" (pronounced like Shawn) will serve as a counterparty, often a seller. This first example will show how trust is an important, but often overlooked, part of most everyday transactions.

Buying a pound of Organic Kenyan Dark Roast coffee

Suppose Bibi wants to buy a pound of Organic Kenyan Dark Roast. She heads down to the local Starbucks to get the coffee, but before she gets there, she runs into Chaun, a stranger who, it just so happens, has a roadside stand that sells one-pound bags labeled "Organic Kenyan Dark Roast Coffee" at half the Starbucks price.

What will Bibi do?

It depends on whether Bibi trusts that Chaun is actually selling authentic Organic Kenyan Dark Roast. For all Bibi knows, Chaun could be selling an inferior grade of coffee, or worse, decaf. Absent trust that the coffee is authentic (organic, Kenyan origin, dark roast), Bibi will likely bypass Chaun's stand and buy the coffee from Starbucks.

How can Bibi know that the coffee Chaun has labeled as "Organic Kenyan Dark Roast" is what it purports to be?

Absent the blockchain trust machine, she can't. What this means for Chaun is that if she wants to sell her coffee, she must give potential customers reasons to trust her product, such as by giving out free samples and showing up week after week to earn customers' confidence. In other words, Chaun must build trust in her product the same way that Starbucks has built trust in its products. That trust, akin to business goodwill, explains the value of brand names, and allows businesses to charge higher prices for their products.

What if Chaun had a way of proving to Bibi the coffee was Organic Kenyan Dark Roast?

If Bibi was confident that the coffee was authentic, she would buy the coffee from Chaun at the lower price. Let's assume Chaun can prove the coffee's provenance, including the source of the beans, which Kenyan farm grew the beans, the "organic" certification of the farm, how long, and at what temperature, the beans were roasted (determinants of "dark" roast), and every transaction and movement from the time the farmer purchased, planted, and harvested the beans until Chaun acquired them.

If that information could be quickly and easily verified, Bibi would buy the coffee from Chaun. That highlights the potential of blockchains: if Bibi could scan a QR code on the bag to review the coffee's provenance on a blockchain, so long as Bibi trusted the information, Bibi would not need to trust Chaun. At that point, Bibi would buy Chaun's coffee because it is cheaper than the coffee from Starbucks.

Bibi might still go to Starbucks, but not to buy bags of Organic Kenyan Dark Roast coffee. If Chaun were successful enough, Starbucks might stop selling that coffee because, with all the overhead of a brick-and-mortar store, Starbucks may not be able to compete with Chaun on the price of Organic Kenyan Dark Roast coffee beans. While Starbucks offers plenty of other desirable things (free Wi-Fi, generally public bathrooms, ready-made drinks, and the ability to create a new name for yourself while waiting for your drink, etc.), it would likely scale down its Organic Kenyan Dark Roast coffee bean business in the locations Chaun has opened stands.

Chaun's side of the transaction involves trust as well. If Bibi pays cash, Chaun must trust that the cash is not counterfeit, albeit a small risk. However, if Bibi pays with a card, multiple forms of trust come into play. The simplest example is if Bibi uses her Visa bank card. When she swipes that card, it is the beginning of the multi-step process described below:

1. The swipe is a request to make a payment from Bibi to Chaun.

2. Chaun submits the request to Visa.

3. Visa sends the request to the financial institution who issued the card to authorize the transaction.

4. If Bibi has enough money in her account (or the financial institution has extended her credit and this payment will not exceed that credit), the financial institution validates the payment and sends an authorization code to Chaun, allowing the transaction to go through.

5.   Chaun accepts the authorization and proceeds with the purchase.

6.   Chaun gives Bibi the coffee.

With Visa (and other credit cards), those processes all happen in a few seconds. But there is a lot more trust involved. First, how does the seller know the person swiping the card is the cardholder? Sellers often don't ask for identification, and for smaller transactions, generally trust the cardholder is authorized to use the card. If the transaction were fraudulent, in general, most US credit card companies would absorb the cost of the fraud and pass it on indirectly through fees to either the customer or the merchant.

How does Chaun know that actual payment is going to be made?

At the time of sale, all Chaun has is an authorization code and a relationship with Visa. Chaun has no relationship with Bibi's financial institution. That means Chaun must trust that (i) the authorization, (ii) her relationship with Visa, and (iii) Visa's relationship with Bibi's financial institution, will ultimately result in Chaun getting paid.

All that trust has a cost. For most credit card transactions, the costs range from 1.5-2.9 percent but can be as high as 3.5 percent. Those fees are generally split between the card issuer (a financial institution) and the card network (Visa). While those percentages seem low, they add up. In the fourth quarter of 2019, Visa processed roughly $2.2 trillion in combined credit and debit card volume, generating revenues of $6.1 billion for the quarter. Those revenues represent the costs of financial intermediation. Blockchain-based payment systems that eliminate legacy financial intermediaries have the potential to reduce or eliminate those costs, returning those revenues to consumers and merchants.

For Visa, its largest expenses are personnel, branding, and fraud detection, which represent over 50 percent of its operating expenses.[1] Bitcoin, the world's most popular blockchain money, has none of those expenses: its personnel work for free, branding is user adoption, and its fraud protection is built in. In fact, while there have been numerous Bitcoin scams, there has *never* been a fake bitcoin created.

The Bitcoin scams that have been reported are generally not threats to the network itself, but instead are (i) schemes to steal a user's bitcoin, (ii) fake crypto exchanges, (iii) pyramid/Ponzi schemes promising "guaranteed" returns, or (iv) some variation of an attempt to employ the greater fool theory (as shown in the figure below).

The Greater Fool Theory

Doing Something Stupid

Hoping Someone Else Is Even More Stupid

Graphic credit: www.scienceabc.com

Of the numerous scams reportedly related to Bitcoin, none have concerned the core Bitcoin blockchain. In fact, when threats to the blockchain have been detected, it has often been Bitcoin's core developers who have detected the threats, and instead of exploiting them, have broadcasted them across the network to solicit help in resolving the errors that created them.

---

[1]   Data from Visa Fiscal Fourth Quarter 2019—Financial Summary and 2018 Annual Report.

Fees on the Bitcoin network

Transactions on the Bitcoin network are not free, but they are far less than the 1.5-3.5 percent fees typical in credit card transactions. In 2019, recording the average transaction on the Bitcoin network required about 250 bytes of data, and the fee for a 1 MB (1 MB = 1,000,000 bytes) block on the network was about $1.89. Doing the math, average Bitcoin transactions cost about $0.0005.

Assuming the lowest credit card transaction fee (1.5 percent), using bitcoin to pay would be about six hundred times cheaper than using Visa for typical transactions. With that lower price, both Bibi and Chaun would prefer that Bibi pay using bitcoin and share the benefit of the lower cost. Moreover, if Bibi later went to Starbucks, Starbucks would also prefer if Bibi paid in bitcoin. In fact, as far back as 2016, Starbucks has allowed their customers to pay with bitcoin using the mobile app IPayYou.

So . . . why isn't everyone using it?

A logical question at this point is, if blockchains are so much cheaper and more efficient, why don't most transactions happen over the blockchain? The simple answer is that blockchain networks are not ready. Yet.

One hurdle blockchain technologies must overcome before widespread adoption is scalability. Right now, even though transactions on the Visa network are about six hundred times more expensive than on the Bitcoin network, Visa can process roughly twenty-four to sixty-five thousand transactions per second, while Bitcoin, the oldest blockchain network, can process fewer than ten transactions per second.

Another hurdle, at least with respect to bitcoin, is price volatility. Over the past few years, the price of one bitcoin (1 BTC) has fluctuated wildly, particularly in 2017. In January 2017, BTC prices hovered around $1,000, but by December 2017, the price reached

$20,000. With such volatility, many are understandably unwilling to use bitcoin for payments (a medium of exchange), and instead acquire and hold bitcoin as a speculative investment asset (a store of value). In the crypto community, slang for holding crypto instead of selling it is called "Hodl," based on a rather infamous typo on a December 2013 Bitcoin Forum message board. Some users have made Hodl an acronym for "Hold On for Dear Life," based on the price volatility of some crypto.

The box below shows an extreme example of the risks of paying with bitcoin.

The two $50 million pizzas

On May 22, 2010, known as "Bitcoin Pizza Day," Florida-based programmer Laszlo Hanyecz wanted two pizzas delivered to his home, and the cost was about twenty-five dollars. Hanyecz went on a Bitcoin forum and asked if anyone would order the pizzas for him in exchange for bitcoin. A British man agreed and paid the pizza joint using a credit card, and Hanyecz sent him 10,000 BTC, at the time worth about $25.

At a January 2020 price of 1 BTC = $10,000,[2] those pizzas cost $50 million apiece. Despite the apparent loss, Hanyecz was untroubled by the transaction, and told the *New York Times*, "It wasn't like bitcoins had any value back then, so the idea of trading them for a pizza was incredibly cool."

Not just money

Although money is the clearest and most accepted application of blockchain technologies, the excitement in the area is not limited

---

[2]   This book uses the January 2020 price of 1 BTC = $10,000 throughout, because it is a nice round number, and there is no telling what the price of bitcoin will be when you read this. Also, if I could predict the price of bitcoin, this book would be called *The Bitcoin Billionaire's Short & Happy Guide to Bitcoin, Blockchain, and Crypto*.

to its use as money. Blockchain technologies, borne out of the financial crisis, have broader goals. According to Vitalik Buterin, the founder of Ethereum (the second most well-known blockchain):

> the idea was to build a new system for everything from payments and banking to health care and identity that was either a replacement for the old one, or at least an alternative to it, one that was borderless, independent of state control and of exploitation by Big Tech . . . The cryptocurrency space has succeeded in making certain aspects of the international economy more open, when politics is moving in the exact opposite direction . . . [and] that's a meaningful contribution to the world.

Ethereum is the world's leading programmable blockchain, and it allows developers to build applications that make use of blockchain technologies (called decentralized applications or "ÐApps") without having to create a new blockchain for every application. Ethereum has a native crypto called Ether (ETH), that like BTC, can be used as digital money. However, because every transaction or operation on the Ethereum network requires some amount of ETH (pronounced "eeth," and often called gas), ETH also serves as a unit of measurement for the computational effort needed to execute operations on Ethereum's network.

As of the end of 2019, Ethereum was the leading ÐApp platform, though it was not the only one. Tron and EOS were Ethereum's most significant challengers, and collectively, the three platforms accounted for over 98 percent of total ÐApp transaction volume.

ÐApps are a critical component in the evolution of the Internet of Things (IoT), which encompasses the network of devices embedded with software, sensors, actuators, and connectivity to the internet which enables those devices to connect and exchange data, thereby creating opportunities for more direct integration of the physical world into computer-based systems. The promise of the IoT is that it will make the devices we use smarter, more efficient, cheaper, and more responsive, and will serve as a bridge to connect the digital and physical universes.

Estimates suggest that by the end of 2020, there will be over 30 billion IoT connected devices. However today, most of those IoT devices rely on centralized communication models, which have high maintenance and infrastructure costs, a central point of failure, and are an attractive target for hackers (a honeypot). Blockchains could reduce or eliminate many of those issues, and allow IoT devices to scale to meet demand.

Blockchain Technologies: A Guide to the Basics

This book provides an overview of blockchain technologies and applications, but is not written to provide the detailed technical specifications used by programmers and developers. However, because so much about the subject matter is technical, this chapter gives readers an overview of certain technical concepts to better understand the mechanics of blockchain applications.

So let's start at the beginning: What is a blockchain?

Many definitions exist for what a blockchain is, and while similar, very few agree to one single definition. Here are a few:

> *A blockchain . . . is a growing list of records, called blocks, which are linked using cryptography.*
> —Wikipedia

> *A mathematical structure for storing data in a way that is nearly impossible to fake. It can be used for all kinds of valuable data.*
> —MIT Technology Review (2018)

> *The blockchain is an incorruptible digital ledger of economic transactions that can be programmed to record not just financial transactions but virtually everything of value."*
> —Don and Alex Tapscott, *Blockchain Revolution* (2016)

> *A blockchain is, in the simplest of terms, a time-stamped series of immutable record of data that is managed by cluster of computers not owned by any single entity. Each of these blocks of data (i.e. block) are secured and bound to each other using cryptographic principles (i.e. chain).*
> —Blockgeeks.com

For this book, the working definition is as follows:

A blockchain is a secure, time-stamped set of immutable individual records (blocks) managed in a decentralized peer-to-peer network of computers (each computer is a node), in which there is agreement to a protocol (a set of rules), for the network that:

- allows digital information to be distributed and viewed (but not copied) across the network;

- is protected using cryptographic principles; and

- permits the creation of new blocks to be added according to a consensus mechanism.

A blockchain's consensus mechanism is structured to verify and ensure:

- there is consensus about the entire history of the blockchain before a new block is added;

- the data in the new block does not conflict with any past data in the blockchain; and

- the actors responsible for adding new blocks to the blockchain are incentivized to act in the best interest of the blockchain and punished for actions contrary to the interests of the network.

That definition may not be perfect, but it works for the vast majority of public blockchains.[3] In order to unpack that definition, some of the terminology used is explained below.

Secure, time-stamped, immutable records. Every historical record on a blockchain includes the exact date and time a transaction was executed, and those historical digital records cannot be changed absent extraordinary

---

[3] Private blockchains are similar to public blockchains, except they are generally not decentralized. Instead, they are often invitation-only networks governed by a centralized entity or group of entities. They allow entities to utilize blockchain technology, but keep the data private.

circumstances. The records are immutable because all computers on the network (nodes) have a copy of all historical transactions (blocks) that anyone can view in real time, and there must be agreement of the state of history before another block can be added to the blockchain. Because those historical blocks are distributed across an entire network of computers, falsifying even one historical record would mean falsifying the entire blockchain.

Decentralized peer-to-peer network. The digital history of the blockchain, which includes records of all previous transactions, are shared among all nodes. That allows the network to be decentralized because no one party or central authority has the power to control the blockchain.

Miners.[4] The combination of special-purpose software, powerfully designed hardware, and users who add blocks to a proof of work blockchain (described below) only after solving a complex cryptographic puzzle.

Node. A device connecting to the blockchain network such as a computer (or phone or printer, so long as it has an IP address and is connected to the internet) that supports the network by (1) maintaining a copy of the blockchain, (2) validating transactions, and sometimes (3) processing transactions. However, not all nodes are the same. Generally, there are two types of nodes:

Full nodes store a copy of the entire blockchain, including all past transactions. Full nodes require a

---

[4]   Miners is used here because they are used in the most popular blockchains, like Bitcoin and Ethereum, that use a proof of work consensus mechanism, described later in the chapter. Other blockchains use different consensus mechanisms that do not rely on miners, and rely on "validators" or "forgers" to add blocks to the blockchain.

lot of storage and memory dedicated to the blockchain.

Light nodes store only a part of the blockchain, typically only the parts of the blockchain the user will need. To ensure the information on a light node is accurate, light nodes often periodically query full nodes to verify the accuracy their information.

Protocol. The set of rules that governs actions on the blockchain. Those rules define what software is used, how the blockchain will operate, and how the nodes will communicate.

Consensus. The problem of reaching consensus among a distributed network of actors has long been an unsolved computer science problem, and, in some respects, Bitcoin solved it. The problem is often represented as the Byzantine Generals' Problem, described below.

The Byzantine Generals' Problem

This situation can be expressed abstractly in terms of a group of generals of the Byzantine army camped with their troops around an enemy city. Communicating only by messenger, the generals must agree upon a common battle plan. However, one or more of them may be traitors who will try to confuse the others, leading to an uncoordinated attack and defeat. The problem is to find an algorithm to ensure that the loyal generals will reach agreement.[5]

---

[5] See Lamport, Shostak, and Pease, *The Byzantine Generals Problem*, ACM (1982).

| Coordinated Attack Leading to Victory | Uncoordinated Attack Leading to Defeat |

Graphic credit: https://medium.com/@paul_12056/byzantine-generals-problem-ff4bdc340e56

The Bitcoin whitepaper[6] provided the first practical solution to the Byzantine Generals' Problem: its proof of work consensus mechanism, described more fully below.

<u>Consensus mechanism</u>

Consensus mechanisms (sometimes called consensus protocols) are the specific rules that determine how a distributed group of nodes reaches consensus on verifying transactions and adding new blocks to the blockchain. Consensus mechanisms try to solve what Vitalik Buterin, the founder of Ethereum, has called the "scalability trilemma," i.e., a protocol that is secure, scalable, and decentralized.

Secure: How immutable and resistant to attack is the blockchain.

Scalable: How many transactions the network can handle, and how quickly it can process those transactions.

---

[6]   See Satoshi Nakamoto, *Bitcoin: A Peer-to-Peer Electronic Cash System* (2008), available at https://bitcoin.org/bitcoin.pdf.

Decentralized: How concentrated is control over the blockchain. Decentralization is a core principle of blockchain technologies, allowing them to be censorship-resistant, and reducing or eliminating central points of failure.

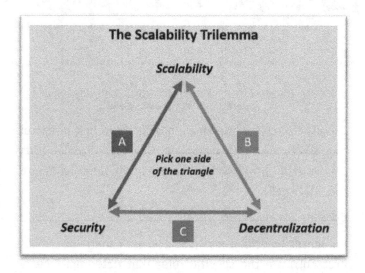

(Image from https://medium.com/logos-network/everything-you-know-about-the-scalability-trilemma-is-probably-wrong-bc4f4b7a7ef.)

Increases in any one corner of the scalability trilemma generally come at the expense of the other two. In many respects, the scalability trilemma is similar to the problem faced by those in need of a home-improvement contractor. Those contractors, by and large, face a similar trilemma: the work can be done fast, cheap, or well. Increases in any two come at the expense of the third.

Consensus Mechanisms

There are three major consensus protocols in use today: proof of work, proof of stake, and delegated proof of stake.

Proof of work (PoW)

PoW is the original consensus protocol and regarded as Bitcoin's greatest innovation because it solved the Byzantine Generals' Problem. PoW is used by both Bitcoin and Ethereum, although Ethereum has announced plans to switch to a proof of stake system in the future.

Generally, in PoW, miners look for transactions broadcast over the network and organize those transactions into blocks. The miners then compete with one another to add their block to the blockchain. The winning miner earns a block reward, which is a set amount of the network's tokens.

The competition involved in the PoW system is that the block reward is awarded only to the first miner to solve a complicated math problem, called a cryptographic hash function. Without going into a rabbit hole of computer science and math, the only way to solve the hash function is by throwing a lot of computing power at it. After several trillion tries of all possible combinations of answers (called brute-force computing), one or more miners will solve the hash function. At that point, the first miner to solve the hash function is chosen to add the next block (if more than one miner solved the hash function, one miner is picked at random to add the next block). Once the new block is added, which happens roughly every 10 minutes in the Bitcoin network, the miners go back to work trying to solve the next hash function.

Why do the miners spend all this computing power trying to solve the hash functions?

Good question. They do it for the block rewards. At the January 2020 price of $10,000 per BTC, the Bitcoin block reward was 12.5 BTC, so each block reward was worth $125,000. Because roughly 144 blocks are added per day, when BTC is trading at $10,000, block rewards generate roughly $14.4 million of value per day. The higher the price of bitcoin, the more incentive miners have to try to solve the hash function. The Bitcoin network has a mechanism in place, called a difficulty adjustment, to change the difficulty of its hash function based on the computing power of active miners working to solve the hash, called the network's hash power. The difficulty adjustment is programmed to adjust every 2016 blocks, or roughly every two weeks, to ensure that the network continues to create new blocks roughly every ten minutes.

Cryptographic principles in PoW

Without diving too deeply into game theory and cryptography, hash functions typically take an input string of any size, perform an operation on that string, and output a unique string of a fixed size. One important property of a hash function is that *any* change to the input string will generate a completely different output string.

An often-used example of a hash function is a website password: you make up a password and enter it, and the website performs a hash function on your password and stores the output of that hash function. The hash function does not care how long your password is, because no matter the length, it will create a unique, fixed number output based on your password, and that output is stored. Then, the next time you try to log on and enter your password, the website runs the same hash function and compares the output with what it has stored. If the output matches, you are able to log on.

> *It's simple ain't it, but quite clever.*
> —Erik B. & Rakim, *Move the Crowd* (1987)

In Bitcoin mining, the hash function is called Secure Hashing Algorithm 256 (SHA-256). The input for SHA-256 includes:

- the data containing the new, not-yet-confirmed transactions grouped together;
- data relating to previous blocks; and

- current time and date information.

The output hash is a unique 256-bit string of data based on those inputs. For security reasons, the protocol often requires double hashing, to ensure that an attacker cannot produce the same hash with a different input. In order to ensure that the hash is sufficiently secure, the Bitcoin network adds some data (a *NONCE*—short for a *Number* that can only be used *ONCE*) to ensure the hash of the block will contain a series of leading zeroes. This is when the miners get to work.

The miners must generate a hash with the correct information about the new block and the *NONCE* so that it matches what the network has produced. The first miner to find that hash, then have it verified and accepted by the network, gets to add the next block and receives the block reward.

So how do the miners find the right NONCE?

Brute force: they program their computers to couple different *NONCEs* with the correct block data until they find a combination with the correct number of leading zeros. In early 2020, Bitcoin required a string of about eighteen leading zeros, and the difficulty of finding the right one was about one in six trillion. Once a solution is found, the miner broadcasts the solution to the other nodes, who must verify it. After the other nodes have verified the solution (achieving consensus), that miner will be entitled to the block reward.

How secure is this?

Very. For now. To "crack" a Bitcoin hash (note: "crack" is used because explaining in detail what hacking Bitcoin means would require an additional chapter), an algorithm would have to use the original data and run 2^{256} computations (that is a 78-digit number, about 115 quattuorvigintillion, give or take). Some have speculated that a supercomputer trying to crack the hash, performing 15 trillion calculations per second, would take about 0.65 billion (yes, that's a billion billion) years to crack it.

A more realistic threat is quantum computers. Current estimates are that it would take "only" 128^3 (about 13.5 million) basic quantum operations to be able to crack a Bitcoin hash. While quantum computers are currently mostly science fiction, current estimates are that by 2027, a quantum computer *could* crack Bitcoin within the ten-minute time period needed to create a new block.

Whether quantum computers pose a real threat to Bitcoin is doubtful. Among the reasons are:

- developers and researchers are already working on quantum-resistant solutions; and

- when quantum computers advance to the point that cracking Bitcoin is possible, quantum cryptography will likely not be far behind to eliminate the threat.

A more practical reason to doubt the threat is that if a quantum computer could crack Bitcoin, it could also crack all other programs and institutions that rely on cryptography, including almost all governments and banks. An attack on those institutions would be a far more financially attractive proposition than an attack on Bitcoin.

Pros and cons of PoW

The most-cited benefits of PoW are:

Decentralization. PoW systems are decentralized because thousands of computers run full nodes, each with a copy of the entire blockchain. In early 2020, estimates indicated there were over eleven thousand full Bitcoin nodes.

Security. PoW networks are believed to be secure because they can only be corrupted by a group of miners who collude and coordinate an attack using 51 percent of the networks' hash power (called a 51 percent attack). A 51 percent attack would allow the colluders to double-spend bitcoins, cancel transactions, and/or transfer others' bitcoins to their own accounts. In April 2020, according to blockchain.com, the two largest Bitcoin mining pools, run by Poolin and F2Pool, controlled roughly 39 percent of Bitcoin's hash power. To launch a 51 percent attack, the top three mining pools (or the right combination of the top four) would have to agree to collude. That scenario is unlikely (though not impossible) because after such an attack was discovered, all tokens would lose value, and other stakeholders in the Bitcoin network (and governments) would likely act to punish the attackers. In effect, an attack on a mature PoW network would cost more money than attacker would be able to steal.

The most-cited costs of PoW are:

Energy Consumption. Many claim that having all those computers solve hash functions wastes energy and is harmful to the environment. Estimates[7] are that Bitcoin's current estimated annual electricity consumption is 69.17 terawatts per year, enough to power 6.4 million US households and the annual energy consumption of the Czech Republic. Whether that energy is wasted, however, is a value judgment. In 2019, global crypto mining revenues were roughly $5.4 billion, and generated over $500 million in profits. In addition, almost 75 percent of the energy required to mine bitcoin came from renewable sources, making it one of the cleanest large-scale industries in the world.

---

[7] The data are available at https://digiconomist.net/bitcoin-energy-consumption.

Scalability. Because full nodes need to reach consensus before a new block can be added, which takes around ten minutes, PoW is slow compared to Visa, as well as some of the other consensus protocols described below.

Incentives. In PoW, only the miners are directly incentivized to secure the network, leaving other stakeholders, such as users and developers, outside the process.

Proof of stake (PoS)

PoS was the first widely adopted alternative process for verifying transactions on the blockchain. In PoS, the creator of a new block (validator or forger) is chosen by an algorithm among a group of people who are able to put up, or stake, some portions of the tokens they hold, akin to a lottery. Validators earn transaction fees for adding new blocks, and the more tokens potential validators stake, the greater their chance of being selected.

Attacks are possible in PoS systems, but under different circumstances than PoW. Some theories suggest a hacker would need as little as one percent of the tokens in circulation to mount an attack. However, in reality, such an attack would be exceedingly difficult to accomplish on a mature blockchain. In addition, in a PoS system, validators have less incentive to launch an attack because they would (1) lose their staked tokens and (2) devalue the tokens they own if the network lost value or was hacked.

Pros and cons of PoS

The most-cited benefits of PoS are:

Scalability & Speed. The entire network is not needed to validate a transaction, only a few validators. That allows the network to process transactions faster.

Energy Consumption and Costs. Because there is no mining, there is also no need to buy and update expensive computers and chips to run mining software. In addition, there is no significant energy consumption required to operate the network.

Incentives. In PoS, anyone willing to stake tokens may earn transaction fees, which widens the group incentivized to secure the network.

The most-cited costs of PoS are:

Centralization and Plutocracy. The Golden Rule applies: those with the most gold make the rules, and often, those rules help them get richer. In PoS, the validators with the most tokens exercise the most power over the network, choosing which transactions to validate. That makes the system more centralized, less robust, and prone to decisions that favor those holding the most tokens.

Nothing-at-Stake Problem. In PoS, if the blockchain forks (more on forks later, but for now, think of it as a temporary split in the blockchain at a time where it is unclear which side of the split is the "right" one), there is no punishment for a validator to work on both sides of the split chain, even if one of those splits was a hack. Conceivably, that would allow validators to spend the same tokens on both sides of the split (double-spend) before the split is resolved. From an economic standpoint, the optimal strategy for validators would be to validate both sides of the fork so that they earn their fees no matter which side of the split ultimately wins. Nevertheless, although that strategy may be optimal for validators, it results in more instability for the network, because it can delay or complicate consensus, and may make it more costly to mount attacks.

Current blockchains that use PoS include Peercoin and Reddcoin. Ethereum has stated that it plans to change to a PoS system in the near future. The chart below, courtesy of Blockgeeks, compares PoW and PoS.

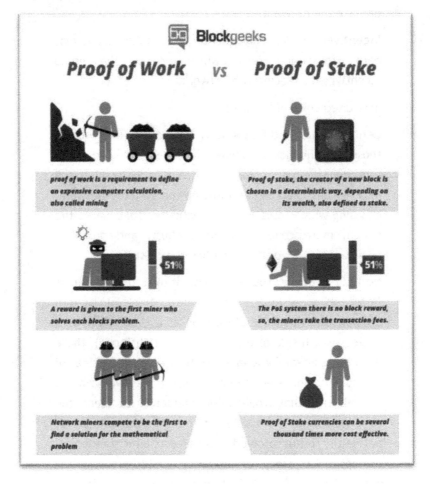

Source: https://blockgeeks.com/.

Delegated proof of stake (DPoS)

DPoS, unsurprisingly, is similar to PoS. However, in DPoS, instead of using tokens to stake, users vote with their tokens to determine which nodes (master nodes) will secure the network. The vote is continual and is based on a one-token, one-vote ("1t1v") system, so the more tokens a user owns, the more voting power and influence she has over the network. Those elected, called delegates or witnesses, get paid for their work in running the master nodes and securing the network.

DPoS users vote based on the reputation of the candidates seeking to be delegates. If at any time a delegate does not do a good job or gets a bad reputation, users can immediately "unelect" that delegate by withdrawing their votes. Because of the power of users to remove poorly performing delegates, the delegates are motivated to keep doing a good job, and that incentive structure is at the heart of DPoS.

The most-cited benefits of DPoS are:

Incentives. Because users choose and retain delegates based on their work and reputation, the delegates are incentivized to do what is best for the users.

Real-Time Voting. Because the blockchain is transparent, users can immediately detect a delegate's bad behavior and vote that delegate out of the system. The potential for the loss of income (and reputation) serves as a motivation.

The most-cited costs of DPoS are:

Centralization Risks. Fewer people in charge means it is easier to coordinate activities among a certain group. An example of that risk occurred in June 2018, when EOS, a DPoS blockchain with only twenty-one delegates, froze the user accounts of seven EOS users suspected of carrying stolen funds. The decision to freeze those accounts was in violation of the rules set forth in EOS's own constitution. That decision, whether justified or not, highlights the risk of giving a small group power over an entire blockchain.

Voter Apathy. DPoS relies on voters who are paying attention. If voters are apathetic, malicious actions by delegates may escape detection.

Centralization and Plutocracy. Because of the 1t1v system, like in PoS, those with more tokens have more influence over the network. As a result, there is a greater chance they may reward and incentivize delegates to act on their behalf at the expense of others.

Current blockchains that use DPoS include BitShares, EOS, Steem, and Tezos.

Blockchain Governance

Blockchain governance describes the process whereby participants agree on a set of parameters for changing the blockchain protocol, resolving disputes, sanctioning rule breakers, and enforcing penalties. For many public blockchains, the goals of its users and developers are not simply to make a profit but, like the internet generally, to create a public good. That creates governance issues.

Most governance mechanisms, however, are ill-suited to deal with economic and social issues together, and often treat them as separate and distinct. A prime example of the failure of governance to deal with economic and social issues is the tragedy of the commons, a situation in which individual users, acting independently according to their own self-interest, behave contrary to the common good of all users by depleting or spoiling a shared resource through their collective actions.

The 2008 financial crisis is a prime example of the failure of business governance mechanisms to consider social welfare. During the crisis, financial institutions, mortgage brokers, real estate agents and others, including some homeowners, engaged in transactions that allowed them to transfer wealth to themselves at the expense of others, including US taxpayers who were left with the bill. The governance mechanisms in place at the time should have worked to combat that type of moral hazard behavior, but in the end, they failed miserably.

It is likely the 2008 financial crisis served as a motivating factor in the creation of Bitcoin. Satoshi Nakamoto, the developer (or developers) of Bitcoin, added only one message onto the first block of Bitcoin mined (the "genesis block") which read:

> The Times 03/Jan/2009 Chancellor on brink of second
> bailout for banks

Many view that message as evidence that Nakamoto's efforts were motivated, or at least influenced, by the financial crisis.

Like in society generally, the choices blockchain stakeholders make regarding economic and social issues are often based on their idiosyncratic incentives. While all stakeholders generally want governance to increase network utility and generate higher token values, different stakeholder groups often want governance to accomplish additional things benefitting them, including:

- users, who want governance to give them more control (often including privacy) over their financial transactions and wealth;

- node operators, who want governance to ensure the costs of running nodes, in terms of both time and equipment, is minimal;

- developers, who want governance to support financial, social and professional recognition for their work, as well as to give them control over the direction of the blockchain; and

- miners and other validators, who want to governance to allow them to minimize their costs and maximize their fees or rewards.

A perfect governance model to satisfy those disparate goals does not exist. For example, although most would agree that network security and scalability are goals of all public blockchains, precisely defining those terms is difficult and involves trade-offs for different stakeholders. Thus, proposed changes require human inputs and a means for the stakeholders to determine the "best" solutions. The means of reaching those solutions is governance.

Fortunately, blockchains allow various types of governance experiments, with fairly low costs of failure. Those failures, however, have created fault lines in the industry, and have often led to contentious blockchain forks and wasted production.

So how are blockchains governed?

Blockchain governance is divided into two camps:

> Off-chain, in which decision-making takes place first on a social level and is later encoded into the protocol by developers; and

> On-chain, in which decision-making rules are encoded into the protocol and any decision that is approved is automatically incorporated into the protocol.

Each shares the same goal—to create a "better" blockchain—but go about it in different ways.

Off-Chain Governance Mechanisms

Off-chain governance mirrors the governance structure of most private institutions. In an off-chain structure, individuals entrusted by the community come together and form a group responsible for blockchain's governance and well-being. That group is tasked with fixing bugs and security vulnerabilities, adding features and improving scalability, representing the blockchain in public discussions, and maintaining the right balance of power among users, developers, miners, and other stakeholders.

One benefit of off-chain governance is informational. So long as responsible and knowledgeable authorities are in charge, they will likely be in the best position to make informed decisions that serve the community's interests. Another benefit involves the decrease in the likelihood of errors because humans can work to correct any code-based errors before they are implemented on the blockchain. However, any off-chain governance process involves a certain amount of centralization, which is contrary to the ethos of the blockchain.

While many off-chain governance mechanisms exist, a useful model is Bitcoin's Bitcoin Improvement Proposal (BIP), if for no other reason than it has existed longer than any other mechanism. The BIP process has been compared to the system of checks and balances in the US government, whereby the developers, like the US Congress, submit proposals (akin to drafting legislation), but others, including the core developers, miners, and node operators (akin, in no particular order, to the executive, the judiciary, and the people) play a role in deciding the merit and propriety of those proposals. Ultimately, however, it is the users (akin to voters) who are the final decision makers, because they can revolt, switch protocols, or sell their tokens if they are unhappy with any changes.

Bitcoin Governance

The BIP process generally begins with a developer submitting an improvement proposal. If deemed worthy, the proposal:

1) becomes a draft;

2) is sent to the Bitcoin core developers for review; and

3) is added to the GitHub repository for BIPs, where it is discussed in the greater community.

Once accepted as a draft, the proposal can be either deferred or withdrawn by the author, or rejected or accepted by the community of node operators. Once a BIP makes it to the "accepted" stage, it cannot be finalized unless miners show 95 percent support for it. Lastly, once finalized, the node operators must upgrade to the new iteration of the protocol, which includes the BIP before the BIP is fully integrated into the Bitcoin blockchain. At the beginning of 2020, there had been approximately 322 BIPs.

The chart below describes the process:

BIP integration process (from Bitcoin Wiki)

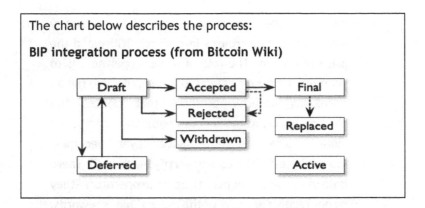

While Bitcoin miners, core developers, and node operators all have incentives to improve the network, those incentives are not often aligned:

- Miners are incentivized to earn block rewards whose value is tied to the price of bitcoin. Many view the miner's incentive structure as Bitcoin's most significant innovation, solving the Byzantine Generals' Problem by paying the generals (here, miners) a salary (the block reward) so long as they act honestly, but garnishing that salary if they are caught trying to cheat.

- Bitcoin developers do not have a direct financial incentive in the price of bitcoin. Instead, as an open-source project, Bitcoin relies on developers who are philosophically aligned with its cypherpunk ethos, believe in the network, and work on it on their own free time. Although Bitcoin developers may not receive direct financial remuneration, they do earn experience and credentials that can be monetized, particularly with the demand for blockchain developers growing exponentially.

- Bitcoin node operators are also indirectly incentivized by increases in network utility and the price of bitcoin. The role of a node operators is to "harness the power of everyday computers to run an overlaying security protocol that polices the blockchain . . . As more nodes enter the system, the more secure the governance layer becomes, increasing efficiencies and fortifying trust."[8] There is no direct financial benefit to node operators—they do not receive any part of the miners' block rewards, nor do they receive the credit for improvements made by the core developers. Their only benefit is increasing the security of the network and, if they own Bitcoin, protection for their investment. Without their participation, the network would come to a grinding halt.

The different stakeholders' incentives help explain why there have been relatively few BIPs implemented (of the 322 BIPs, only approximately 40 had been implemented as of January 2020), and many have been hotly contested.

On-Chain Governance Mechanisms

On-chain governance is a formal system that determines changes to the protocol on the blockchain itself. Most on-chain voting mechanisms allocate decision-making to holders of native tokens on the blockchain. Those mechanisms are often based on a 1t1v mechanism or some derivation thereof, or a "stake-based governance" system whereby, in general, token holders must put some tokens at risk in order to have a role in governance. In either

---

[8]   Rob Viglione (co-founder of ZenCash), *The Benefits of Incentivizing Node Operators in Public Blockchains*, Bitcoin Magazine (May 25, 2018).

case, decisions that are approved are automatically encoded into the protocol.

Tezos is one of the more established blockchains that uses on-chain governance. Its governance process is described briefly below:

Tezos

Tezos describes itself as a "platform to create smart contracts and build decentralized applications that cannot be censored or shut-down by third parties." In Tezos, all stakeholders are permitted to participate in governance, and the protocol provides an election cycle that "provides a formal and systematic procedure for stakeholders to reach agreement on proposed protocol amendments." Tezos also incorporates an explicit improvement mechanism into the blockchain, providing developers with a clear reward framework, and giving token holders the ability to evaluate the merits of a proposal and determine whether the proposal will improve the protocol.

A number of problems with on-chain governance have been identified. A full-throated exploration of those problems is beyond the scope of this book, but some frequently discussed problems are as follows:

- **Plutocracy and Collusion.** A plutocracy is a government by the wealthy. In an on-chain system, a plutocracy indicates control by individuals or entities who hold a significant percentage of the tokens, which allows them to collude and act primarily in their own interest, to the detriment of those with fewer resources.

- **Mutability.** One of the most important features of blockchain technologies is the inability to change transactions recorded on what is supposed to be a permanent ledger. In an on-chain governance system, a vote can be taken to "undo" a transaction or series of transactions and roll back, or edit, the history of the ledger.

- **Excluded Stakeholders.** In many on-chain governance systems, non-token holders are excluded from governance. However, by excluding them, their participation in governance removes an important check to token holders' balance of power, particularly in blockchain applications that do not require users to own tokens.

One blockchain, Decred, uses both on-chain and off-chain governance, and its governance process is described briefly below:

Decred

 Decred describes itself as "open, progressive, and self-funding cryptocurrency with a system of community-based governance integrated into its blockchain." In Decred, holders of tokens can time-lock (stake) their tokens in exchange for tickets, which allow ticket holders to participate in governance in two on-chain and one off-chain governance mechanisms. The on-chain portion allows votes to (1) approve or reject, with a 75 percent approval rating, a proposed change to the consensus rules of the protocol, and (2) approve the work of the miners, which will allow the miners to earn their block reward.

Smart Contracts and Decentralized Applications

Smart Contracts

Smart contracts are blockchain applications that contain a set of rules by which parties can make transactional agreements.[9] Once the conditions to those agreements are met, the terms of the agreement are automatically implemented either on a blockchain or through an off-chain application that relies on a blockchain.

The goal of a smart contract is to set the terms of an agreement and the rules of its enforcement in computer code, thus eliminating the need for trusted intermediaries. A simple example of a non-blockchain smart contract is a vending machine: the rules of the transaction are programmed into the machine. Once the buyer puts the correct amount of money into the machine, the machine confirms the amount is correct and provides the goods.

Although called smart contracts, most are not legal contracts. Rather, they are a set of conditional instructions setting forth rules for performance. Programmed correctly, smart contracts are self-verifying, self-executing, tamper resistant, and in most circumstances can lower transaction costs by reducing or eliminating the need for trusted intermediaries. Ethereum was the first blockchain designed specifically for smart contract development, to create:

> *a platform that could sustain not only the money or medium of exchange use case, but also to add programmability to money, introducing conditional logic to the equation that would open up a world of possibilities with regards to decentralized financial*

---

[9]　The term *smart contract* was coined in 1993 by Nick Szabo, a computer scientist, legal scholar, and cryptographer, while researching the ambiguities of language in an effort to devise a system to allow contract language to be converted into computer code.

applications and products, and additional decentralized applications.[10]

Ethereum: A Smart Contract Platform

In November 2013, Vitalik Buterin distributed the Ethereum white paper proposing Ethereum as an open-source, distributed computing platform upon which smart contracts, as well as other coins and applications, could be built and maintained. The fuel to run that platform was dubbed "ether," and it is the cryptoasset needed to run programs and store data on the Ethereum system. Ethereum is supported by the non-profit Ethereum Foundation, headquartered in Zug, Switzerland, whose mission includes improving communications to the general public about the progress and development of the Ethereum platform.

The example below explains how a smart contract works.

Blockchain smart contract: wager on the NCAA Championship

 Assume it is the final game of a future (202X) NCAA basketball tournament, and Bibi and Chaun, who do not know each other, want to bet on the outcome. Each wants to bet $100 on the NCAA championship. Bibi wants to bet that the University of Maryland Terrapins (Terps) will win, and Chaun, for some reason (a move to NC?), wants to bet that Duke will win. They both believe if they win, their bet should pay double (two-to-one odds—an "even money" bet). If Maryland wins, Bibi would get $200 (the original $100 bet and an additional $100), and if Duke wins, Chaun would

---

[10] See EthHub, *History and Network Upgrades*, available at https://docs.ethhub.io/ethereum-basics/history-and-forks/.

get $200. Because there are no ties in championship games, absent some catastrophic event, there can only be two results: the Terps win or Duke wins.

Because Bibi and Chaun don't know each other, they need a trusted intermediary to place their bets. That intermediary will serve two important functions: (1) let them know the odds of the bet (here even money) and (2) guarantee payment for a winning bet. For those services, the trusted intermediary will charge a small fee.

In the real world, that trusted intermediary is a bookmaker (bookie), who broadcasts the odds to all potential bettors and tries to find bettors who take offsetting positions, eliminating the bookie's risk. In our scenario, the bookie would inform both Bibi and Chaun that even though it is an even money bet, the bookie is going to charge them a small fee if they win. That fee in gambling parlance is called the "vig" (short for the Yiddish slang *vigorish*),[11] and is generally around 10 percent of the amount of the bet.

Once the game is over and the Terps have won (author's prerogative), Bibi will want to get paid for her winning bet. The bookie will then give Bibi $190, equal to the $100 originally bet plus the $100 winnings minus the $10 vig (10 percent of $100).

Here is where smart contracts can add value. Under the same terms, both Bibi and Chaun would have been better off placing their bets directly with each other through a smart contract that did not charge a 10 percent vig.

That contract would be structured to:

- broadcast that there is a smart contract for people who want to make bets on the NCAA championship;

---

[11] The word traces its origins to the Russian word выигрыш, romanized as výigryš, meaning gain or winnings.

- match bettors who take offsetting odds, like Bibi and Chaun;

- provide a mechanism for those betters to enter into a smart contract for their bets;

- collect the wagered funds from each bettor and hold those funds in the smart contract until the game is over; and

- pay the winner all the funds held in the smart contract, minus a tiny (fraction of a penny) blockchain transaction cost.

The smart contract performs all the tasks that the bookie did but at a much lower cost. But that raises a practical question:

How will the smart contract know who won?

Just like Morpheus and Neo in the *Matrix*, the smart contract needs to see the Oracle.

Oracles

An oracle is a program, device, or entity that provides external data to smart contracts to determine if conditions have (or have not) been satisfied, without violating the integrity of the blockchain. In a smart contract, an oracle finds and verifies real-world occurrences, then sends that information to either a blockchain to be used by smart contracts or directly to a smart contract.

Why should the oracle be trusted?

Because blockchain systems are designed to be trustless, oracles introduce some level of trust, and therefore some level of risk, back into the system. However, an evolving set of oracles has evolved to reduce the vulnerabilities associated with using oracles through financial, reputation, and governance protocols. In addition, many smart contracts rely on multiple oracles to further reduce those vulnerabilities.

In an article in Hacker Noon,[12] Jesus Rodrigues presented a basic taxonomy of oracles, described below:

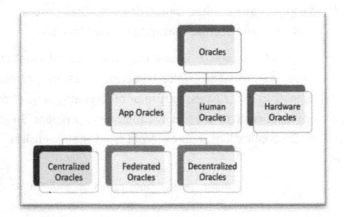

<u>Human Oracles</u>: Individuals or groups who access and enter external data into a blockchain.

<u>App Oracles</u>: Software applications that capture data directly from the internet or through online application programming interfaces (APIs) and transmits the data to blockchain applications. Of the App Oracles, there are three basic types:

1) **Centralized Oracles** that rely on information from APIs or other centralized applications;

2) **Federated Oracles** that rely on a small number of nodes to validate external information to relate to the main data provider; and

3) **Decentralized Oracles** that collect external data, but before providing it to the blockchain,

---

[12] Jesus Rodrigues, *The Middleman of Trust: The Oracle Paradox and Five Protocols that can Bring External Data into the. . .,* Hacker Noon (July 31, 2018).

validate the data through one or more decentralized consensus protocols.

<u>Hardware Oracles</u>: Electronic devices that capture external data and provide that data to the blockchain.

The challenge of any oracle is ensuring that the information it provides can be trusted. While oracles certainly introduce vulnerabilities into the trustless nature of blockchains, a number of applications have come online to solve the oracle problem. Some of the top oracle applications, and excerpts from their websites, are below:

 Augur (augur.net) relies on individuals to report external events relevant to specific predictions and employs validation-dispute protocols and reputation tokens to maintain a record of an oracle's behavior.

 Chainlink (chain.link) maintains a decentralized oracle network to provide security guarantees as smart contracts themselves. By allowing multiple Chainlinks to evaluate data, Chainlink's application seeks to eliminate points of failure and maintain the overall value of a smart contracts.

 Provable (provable.xyz) provides a platform that allows for integration of multiple data sources as oracles, employs mechanisms called "authenticity proofs" to provide transparency to their processes, and provides a full audit trail for external data provided to smart contracts.

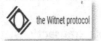 Witnet (witnet.io) is a decentralized oracle network that connects smart contracts to the outer world. It aims to allow any piece of software to retrieve the contents published at any web address with complete and verifiable proof of its integrity and without blindly trusting any third party.

In our example, assume the oracle operates by checking the final score of the game on every major newspaper in the US as well as the top fifty sports-related websites around the world. It also contacts twenty trusted individuals to confirm the information's accuracy. If all parties confirm the score, the oracle would provide the information to the smart contract, telling the smart contract that Maryland won and Duke lost. The smart contract would then make the payout to Bibi.

Diagram of a smart contract[13]

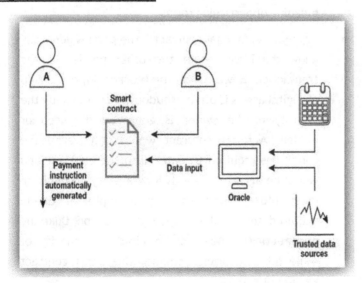

---

[13] Clifford Chance, *Smart Contracts: Legal Framework and Proposed Guidelines for Lawmakers* (Oct. 2018).

Challenges facing smart contracts

The appeal of smart contracts is that for simple transactions, they obviate the need for trusted intermediaries, particularly when the terms of the agreement are fairly straightforward and easily verifiable. However, for more complicated agreements, smart contracts fail to address a number of critical issues, including:

- **Jurisdiction.** Legal contracts are governed according to the law of particular legal or administrative bodies, and those bodies have the authority to resolve controversies arising out of those contracts. In addition, because words mean different things in different contexts, many jurisdictions provide information about the meaning of words used in contracts. Smart contracts, in contrast, often simply set forth the terms of the transactional agreement and are silent with respect to jurisdiction or the meaning of particular terms.

- **Anonymity.** In legal contracts, the parties generally know the identities of the other parties to the transaction. However, on the blockchain, ownership of digital assets is often pseudonymous, meaning the identity of the owner is generally disguised or hidden. A smart contract would only verify the conditions required to enter into the contract and would be agnostic towards how a party was able to meet those conditions. For example, if Chaun acquired the $100 to place the bet on Duke by misdirecting money from a children's charity or some other nefarious scheme, the smart contract would not care.

- **Enforcement of Disputes.** In the event there is a dispute in a legal contract, the parties to that contract can resolve their dispute based on the language of the contract and the rules of the jurisdiction governing the contract. Once that dispute is resolved, a party entitled to a remedy can enforce that remedy according to what is provided in the contract and the laws or rules of the jurisdiction. In a smart contract, if a dispute arises after the smart contract has been executed, there may be no way of identifying other parties to the smart contract. And even if those parties could be identified, absent language in the smart contract setting forth a dispute resolution mechanism, it would be unclear what jurisdiction (i) would have the authority to resolve such a dispute, or (ii) could enforce a remedy.

Some have theorized that smart contracts will someday replace lawyers. That is unlikely. While smart contracts may reduce the demand for some legal practice areas, they will increase the demand for lawyers who can coordinate with coders to draft more sophisticated and robust smart contracts, particularly as more IoT products come online.

Decentralized Applications (ÐApps)

ÐApps are applications that run on a peer-to-peer (P2P) network of computers, and generally allow for the transfer of data. Blockchain ÐApps use the blockchain to allow for the transfer of digital data. Examples of non-blockchain ÐApps include Napster, BitTorrent, and the Tor browser, which are all ÐApps that allow users to exchange data, but do not store that data in any centralized location. Both Bitcoin and Ethereum are examples of ÐApps.

Blockchain ÐApps using smart contracts generally meet the following four criteria:

1. **Open Source.** The source code of ÐApp protocols are available to anyone and operate autonomously.

2. **Decentralized.** ÐApps run on P2P networks that utilize cryptographic technology to store data and avoid central points of failure.

3. **Token Operation.** ÐApps use tokens that are required for the ÐApp to operate. In general, any contribution of value to a ÐApp protocol, such as validating transactions pursuant to the consensus mechanism, is rewarded with a ÐApp's tokens.

4. **Token Generation.** ÐApps generate tokens through its protocol and have a fixed consensus mechanism.

ÐApps generally use either the PoW or PoS consensus mechanism, or a combination of both. As ÐApps evolve, the consensus mechanisms will likely follow suit.

In general, ÐApps fall into three operational categories:

Type 1:   ÐApps with their own blockchain, such as Bitcoin or Ethereum

Type 2:   ÐApps that use the blockchains of Type 1 ÐApps and require tokens to function

Type 3:   ÐApps that use Type 2 ÐApps, but also generally issue and require tokens on their own

One way to think about the different types of ÐApps (ignoring the use of tokens) is:

- Type 1 ÐApps are akin to operating systems, like Microsoft Windows, Android, or Apple's IOS;

- Type 2 ÐApps are akin to software programs that function in an operating system, like Microsoft Word or Adobe Photoshop; and

- Type 3 ÐApps are akin to specialized software that operate inside of other software, like the spellchecker in Microsoft Word.

ÐApp and Smart Contract Platforms

Both ÐApps and smart contracts need a blockchain to operate, and different blockchains have different strengths and weaknesses as ÐApp or smart contract platforms. Often, the main issue is scalability—the ability of the ÐApp or smart contract to carry out transactions quickly.

While Bitcoin has the technological capacity to function as a smart contract platform, its primary function to date has been as a form of money. Other blockchains have sought to provide more functionality for ÐApps or smart contracts, and Ethereum has been the most popular smart contract platform, at least through the first quarter of 2020. According to Ethereum.org:

> "Ethereum is a decentralized platform that runs smart contracts: applications that run exactly as programmed without any possibility of downtime, censorship, fraud or third-party interference," and its coin, ether (ETH) "is a necessary element—a fuel—for operating the distributed application platform Ethereum. It is a form of payment made by the clients of the platform to the machines executing the requested operations."

Ethereum was designed to make building smart contracts and ÐApps easier for developers and entrepreneurs. In 2017-18, 91 percent of all initial coin offerings (ICOs), a form of smart contract, were launched on Ethereum. At the end of 2019, Ethereum, EOS and Tron had over a 98 percent share of total ÐApp transactions, with reported transaction volumes of $12.8 billion, $6.1 billion, and $4.4 billion, respectively.

All face a number of challengers claiming that their networks are "better" for ÐApps and smart contracts, which generally means those networks are faster, more scalable, and can handle more transactions. The scalability problem for Ethereum became apparent in 2017 based on an Ethereum-based ÐApp game *Cryptokitties*.

Cryptokitties

Cryptokitties is a virtual collectibles application that allows users to adopt, raise, and trade virtual cats. *Cryptokitties* relies on a genetic algorithm to spawn new kitties, taking into account parental selection, mutation of genes, and the crossover of genes from each parent, so that each new kitty has a unique genome. In the game, each cryptokitty has a 256-bit genome, which means there are roughly four billion possible genetic variations for each kitty. Also, each kitty is a one-of-a-kind digital asset, because each kitty is represented by a token (called an ERC-721 token) that is nonfungible, meaning each token is unique.

Credit: *Cryptokitties.co.*

In Cryptokitties, smart contracts are used to perform the tasks of breeding, raising, feeding, accessorizing, buying, and selling the kitties. Whenever a new task is performed (such as breeding a new kitty), a new smart contract is executed that inherits information from other related smart contracts (such as each parent's genome). Then, when other tasks need to be performed (such as raising the new kitty), another new smart contract is executed based on the earlier smart contracts. As a blockchain application, the entire smart contract history of each cryptokitty is recorded and available for all to see.

The chart below shows some of the information recorded and the smart contract programming language used:

genes	The genetic code of the kitty.
birthTime	The exact timestamp of the kitty's birth.
cooldownEndBlock	The minimum time that a kitty has to wait before it can breed again
matronId	The ID of the cat's mother
sireId	The ID of the cat's father
siringWithId	If the cat isn't pregnant then this is set to 0. However, if pregnant then this is set to the Id of the father
cooldownIndes	How much longer the cat has to wait before it can breed again.
generation	The generation of the cat. The first kitties produced were generation 0

Source: https://blockgeeks.com/guides/cryptokitties/.

Cryptokitties was the most popular application on Ethereum—so popular, in fact, that it almost shut the network down.

How did Cryptokitties almost shut down Ethereum?

Because breeding, raising, feeding, accessorizing, buying and selling Cryptokitties are all separate smart contracts, at its peak, those activities consumed upwards of 20 percent of Ethereum's network traffic. As a result, transaction processing times went up from a few seconds to ten minutes or more, and many transactions were never executed.

The attraction of *Cryptokitties* and Bitcoin are based on the same principle: scarcity. With Bitcoin, there will only be 21 million BTC ever produced, and that scarcity drives demand. With *Cryptokitties*, it is being able to acquire a unique, and thereby scarce, collectible asset. What *Cryptokitties* developers figured out was that by creating an almost infinite number of traits, the market would continually create demand for certain traits, and users would get hooked on breeding, trading and collecting kitties with those traits. The network problems with *Cryptokitties* highlighted one of the major roadblocks to widespread blockchain adoption: scalability.

Scalability

For a blockchain application to reach mainstream users, it has to perform like mainstream applications. In a world with the internet and 5G, that means fast. But most major blockchains, because of the scalability trilemma, cannot execute transactions quickly without compromising security and decentralization. For PoW blockchains, speed is determined by two primary factors: the time to add a transaction to a block and the time to reach consensus.

Scalability problems on PoW blockchains present a difficult technological challenge. Currently, many blockchain nodes store the entire history of the blockchain and, in some cases, also process transactions. The two most popular PoW blockchains, Bitcoin and Ethereum, can process only between three-to-seven and seven-to-fifteen transactions per second, respectively,[14] far less than Visa's twenty-four thousand transactions per second. That inability to scale presents a challenge to widespread adoption.

One factor that limits Bitcoin's ability to process transactions at scale (transactional throughput) is the amount of data in each block. Currently, Bitcoin has a 1 MB block size limit.[15] One much debated Bitcoin scalability solution has been to increase the base block size, allowing more transactions to be included in each block. In that debate, the primary argument for increasing the block size was that doing so would permit more data to be included in each block, allowing for greater transactional throughput. The primary argument against increasing the block size was that it would put the costs of scaling directly onto node operators, who would have to upgrade their equipment to account for the computational and storage needs of larger blocks. As more node operators opted out,

---

[14] These end-of-2019 estimates of transactional throughput are based on average sized transactions.

[15] Originally, Bitcoin did not have a block size limit. However, in March 2010, Satoshi Nakamoto explicitly limited the block size to 1 MB.

because they were either unable or unwilling to upgrade, the network would necessarily become more centralized.

The first Bitcoin debate about increasing the block size played out in 2015. The Bitcoin community ultimately decided not to increase the block size, which led to a chain split in which the blockchain was forked into two separate chains: the original Bitcoin blockchain and a new blockchain called Bitcoin Cash (BCH), all discussed later in this chapter.

Some scaling solutions have been, or soon will be, implemented that allow only a subset of nodes to verify transactions. To date, the most discussed of those solutions are SegWit and Lightning on Bitcoin, and Sharding and Plasma on Ethereum.

Different solutions have evolved on each chain because, broadly speaking, each chain serves a different goal: Bitcoin's value proposition is its role as "digital gold," a crypto that acts as primarily as a store of value, but can also serve as a medium of exchange and unit of account (as discussed in Part II). Ethereum's value proposition is as the operating system for a broad array of smart contracts and ÐApps, and potentially the main operating system for the IoT.

Bitcoin Scaling—SegWit and Lightning

SegWit

SegWit was a BIP (BIP 141) intended to mitigate Bitcoin block size limitation problems and address other technical issues. When SegWit was activated in August 2017, it increased block capacity and allowed more transactions to be processed using the same amount of data. SegWit, short for segregated witnesses, accomplished this by separating two key components of data recorded on the blockchain. SegWit also provided a "malleability fix" to the network which made

it more difficult to tamper with transaction identities. Without that SegWit malleability fix, the Lightning Network, described below, would not have been possible.

How does SegWit work?

Blockchain transactions include both signature data, which verifies the sender has the funds to make a payment (called the "witness" information), as well as transactional data, which details the contemplated transaction. SegWit segregates that signature data (the witness information) from the transactional data. Because signature data make up roughly 65 percent of the data in a typical transaction, SegWit greatly reduced the amount of data needed to consummate a transaction, allowing more transactions to fit into each block, thereby increasing the blockchain's transactional capacity. Broadly speaking, SegWit allows a 1 MB Bitcoin block to perform like a more secure 4 MB block.

Although SegWit appears to have reduced Bitcoin's scalability problems, its implementation was not without controversy. Without delving into the technical details, removing the witness data from a block could make it more difficult to demonstrate a transaction actually happened. The disagreements regarding SegWit was one of the factors that led to the first contentious Bitcoin chain split and the creation of Bitcoin Cash (BCH).

As discussed above, at around the time of the integration of SegWit, some in the Bitcoin community believed a better solution to scaling was to increase the block size. After a very public debate, however, the Bitcoin community decided not to increase the block size and only implement SegWit. That decision caused a group of miners, developers, and activists to fork the Bitcoin blockchain and split off at a point before SegWit was implemented. The new chain, called Bitcoin Cash, had the same pre-SegWit history of Bitcoin, but allowed for up to an 8 MB block size (compared to 1 MB for Bitcoin).

After the hard fork, anyone who owned BTC also owned an identical amount of BCH.

Lightning

The Lightning Network is a second layer protocol[16] that offers another solution to the Bitcoin scalability problem. Lightning works by:

- identifying a portion of relevant data from the blockchain;

- moving that data off the blockchain (off-chain);

- executing transactions using that off-chain data;

- reconciling all the off-chain transactions; and

- integrating the reconciled transactions back onto the blockchain.

Individual transactions using the Lightning Network (Lightning transactions) are not recorded on the blockchain (on-chain), which frees up the blockchain to perform other tasks. Instead, those Lightning transactions are verified and recorded off-chain, and at some later point, the net result of those Lightning transactions are reconciled on-chain.

Lightning works by allowing users to open second layer payment channels, then executing transactions off-chain using those channels. Once all the transactions for a particular channel are completed, those payments are netted and reconciled, and the channel is closed. Once closed, the record of all the transactions in the channel while it was open are reconciled and recorded on-chain.

---

[16] Generally, a second layer protocol is built to run "on top of" an existing blockchain, using a second layer of smart contracts over the main blockchain.

An example of Lightning Network transactions

Assume Bibi and Chaun regularly bought and sold goods to each other. To avoid recording each transaction on the blockchain, they could set up a payment channel by each of them moving $100 from the blockchain to their payment channel. At that point, they could buy and sell with each other using their payment channel, without the need to record each transaction on the blockchain.

It would work like this, assuming they both open a four-day payment channel on Sunday and moved $100 each onto the channel:

- On Monday, Bibi sends Chaun $40.
- On Tuesday, Chaun sends Bibi $50.
- On Wednesday, they close the channel.

Once the channel is closed, the payments would be netted:

- Bibi: $100 – $40 + $50 = $110.
- Chaun: $100 + $40 – $50 = $90.

The information from the closed channel would be sent back to the blockchain with instructions to send $110 to Bibi's account, and $90 to Chaun's account. The benefit of the Lightning network is it obviates the need for the network to record and verify the underlying Monday and Tuesday transactions.

Many see Lightning as a way to allow bitcoin to be used to make everyday transactions. The benefits include lower transactions costs, as the entire network does not need to handle each transaction, and greater network capacity, as these off-chain transactions will not clog up the network and allow more transactions to be processed. That capacity is most beneficial for microtransactions and IoT uses, in which instructions can be sent to internet-connected devices to perform certain tasks.

According to 1ML, a Lightning Network search and analysis engine, at the end of 2019, the Lightning Network had a network capacity of roughly 850 BTC, eleven thousand nodes, and thirty-five thousand payment channels and a median base fee of 1 Satoshi (one-hundred millionth of a bitcoin). However, as with most things in life, the devil is in the details. A few of the problems identified in the Lightning network are as follows:

- *Locked-up funds.* As shown in the previous example, Lightning Network users need to deposit funds in a channel, which means those funds are locked up on the channel until it closes. The longer a channel is open and the more transactions it executes, the more efficient it is at getting transactions off the blockchain and making the network more efficient. However, that also increases the risk of changing prices. For example, if a user has a channel that stays open for one week and wants to sell because the price of BTC crashes for some reason, that user is locked in until the channel closes.

- *Centralization.* Whether Lightning will increase centralization, thereby making the network generally less secure and more vulnerable to attack, is a much-debated question. The centralization argument is based, in part, on the belief that what will evolve is a form of hub-and-spoke centralization (Figure A).

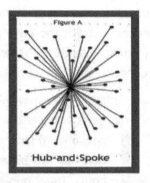

In a nutshell, this argument claims that to connect different users with different channels, what will emerge is a hub-and-spoke system where many users connect to the same hubs so that they can transact with one another. Thus, those hubs will be easier to attack, and the parties in control of the payment channels operating those hubs will have too much control over the network.

Others argue that the risk of hub and spoke centralization is overblown, and what will likely emerge is a form of a hot potato distributed network (Figure B). In a nutshell, in a hot potato distributed

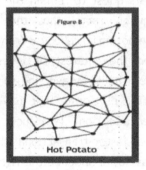

network, each node passes a transaction to the next node willing to take the transaction closer to its destination, using what is called source and onion routing. Source routing means the payment sender constructs the route of the payment. Onion routing means that for multi-hop transactions (hot potatoes), the intermediate nodes along the way only know the identities of two parties: the party that transferred the payment in and the next party to receive the payment. The ultimate destination will be the only node that knows the payment will stop there. Source and onion routing allow the source and ultimate destination of the payment to track the payment, while still protecting their identities, thereby enhancing privacy and censorship resistance.

The answer, as with many things in life, may fall in the middle. What may emerge is a decentralized

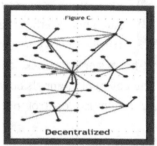

network (Figure C) that has attributes of both the hub-and-spoke centralization in Figure A and the hot potato distributed networks in Figure B.

Ethereum Scaling

Ethereum has been more aggressive in attempting to scale because it faces greater competition in its quest to remain the dominant platform for ÐApps and smart contracts, thus the dominant operating system for the IoT. The potential revenues from usurping Ethereum's position has piqued the interest of investors and developers alike, and has allowed them, by avoiding some of the limitations of Ethereum, to offer platforms that have greater potential for scaling and wider adoption. Two such Ethereum competitors, EOS and Tron, claim faster transactional throughput and lower fees. But Ethereum has not abandoned the fight and has taken significant steps to improve.

Ethereum's most discussed scaling improvements are the Raiden Network, Plasma, Sharding, planned forks (including Constantinople, Istanbul, and Berlin) and Casper—Ethereum's proposed change to a PoS consensus mechanism. The name for the full integration of Casper and Sharding is "Serenity" and it will create what has been dubbed "Ethereum 2.0." Each is discussed briefly below.

Raiden Network and Plasma

The Raiden Network is essentially Ethereum's version of the Lightning Network, and it went live on Ethereum's main network in December 2018. Like Lightning, Plasma sends transactions off-chain while relying on the Ethereum network for its underlying security. However, Plasma's architecture is structured more like a tree, with branches off the main Ethereum blockchain that can spawn other branches. Plasma works by moving the computationally complex transactions to the side branches and only broadcasting the completed smart contracts to the Ethereum blockchain.

Sharding

Sharding is a concept widely used in databases to make them more efficient. A shard is a horizontal portion, or slice, of a database. Sharding works by partitioning large databases into smaller databases, which makes performing database operations more manageable.

For blockchains, sharding works by partitioning the existing blockchain into smaller pieces (shards) so that each node need only store a shard of the blockchain's data, but allows the shards to communicate in a way that will allow the chain to remain secure and decentralized. By some estimates, if Ethereum had one hundred shards, the chain would be able to process around ten thousand transactions per second. However, Ethereum cannot use sharding until Casper is implemented, because sharding in a PoW network is more difficult and makes the network more vulnerable to attack.

Although sharding offers many potential benefits, it also exposes a number of potential attack vectors. Generally speaking, those vectors relate to the data validity and availability:

Validity: When interacting with a shard, it may be impossible to validate the history of that shard, which puts into question the validity of the entire chain that shard claims to represent.

Availability: A full explanation of the data availability problem is beyond the scope of this book. Very briefly, the problem has to do with ensuring there is sufficient data in shards to detect attacks and fraud, allowing transactions to be either (i) deemed verified and processed, or (ii) deemed invalid and penalized, thereby disincentivizing future attacks and fraudulent activities.

Planned Ethereum Forks

Many improvements to Ethereum are implemented through planned software upgrades, called forks. Some of the more significant planned forks are described below:

Constantinople: Constantinople was a February 2019, upgrade to Ethereum that was designed to, among other things, make it easier to develop projects on the chain, allow implementation of scaling solutions in the future, and be a step toward transitioning Ethereum to a PoS chain (Casper). Constantinople required a hard fork of the Ethereum blockchain and reduced the block reward from 3 ETC to 2 ETC (the previous major fork upgrade, Byzantium, reduced the block reward from 5 ETC to 3 ETC).

Istanbul: Istanbul was a December 2019 hard fork that introduced additional privacy and scaling capabilities, rebalanced certain ETH pricing mechanisms, allowed Ethereum and Zcash (a crypto that offers completely private transactions that can be verified by smart contracts on Ethereum) to work better together, and permitted more functionality to smart contracts.

Berlin: The Berlin hard fork is tentatively expected in June 2020, and will introduce an algorithm dubbed Progressive Proof of Work (ProgPoW). As explained by CoinDesk, ProgPoW is a transitional step needed before Ethereum changes to a PoS system. In addition, Berlin will reduce the mining capabilities of the more expensive ASIC chips (ASIC chips are "application-specific integrated circuits" which are computer chips specially designed for, and therefore thousands of times more efficient at, mining) and increase the capabilities of non-ASIC chips used in most personal computers, like CPUs and GPUs (GPUs are "graphics processing units" which are found in many standard computers and allow images to be displayed). One reason for the move away from ASIC chips is the belief that as more mining is done by ASIC chips, fewer miners will be able to compete for block rewards, and the mining pool will become more centralized.

Casper: Ethereum's most profound change will be Casper, which will transition Ethereum to a PoS chain. Doing so would eliminate Ethereum mining and, by moving to PoS, allow much faster transactional throughput.

Serenity—Ethereum 2.0

Serenity is the final step in Ethereum 2.0 and a combination of Casper and Sharding that cannot be implemented until both are operational. Serenity is not expected to be implemented until late 2020 at the earliest. According to the Ethereum core developers, Serenity will complete the switch to a PoS consensus mechanism and usher in a thousand-fold increase in scalability, while also making the chain more secure and energy efficient.

Forks and Chain Splits

Not everything that is faced can be changed, but nothing can be changed until it is faced.
—James Baldwin

There often comes a time when, for one reason or another, things change. On the blockchain, those changes are represented by forks. A blockchain fork is a modification of the blockchain's software, and a forked blockchain refers to a blockchain after the modification has been implemented.

Much has been written about some of the more contentious forks in Bitcoin and Ethereum, but forks are sometimes benign. In some cases, a fork occurs when two or more nodes discover blocks at the same time. These forks are temporary and resolved on the blockchain. In other cases, forks are used to implement upgrades or to test features and processes on a blockchain before introducing them to the public.

There are two types of forks: hard forks and soft forks. The primary difference between the two deals with backwards compatibility, which is the ability of new versions of the blockchain to understand and function on data created by older versions of the blockchain. Each is discussed below.

Soft fork

A soft fork is a software upgrade that tightens or restricts the rules of the protocol. Soft forks are backwards compatible, meaning older pre-fork blocks can accept and work with newer post-fork blocks. However, the newer post-fork blocks would reject the older pre-fork blocks if those older pre-fork blocks violate the rules instituted by the soft fork.

An example of a soft fork was Bitcoin's introduction of a block size limit. Initially, Bitcoin did not have a limit on the size of a block, but a soft fork was executed in 2010 that set a 1 MB block size limit for all new blocks. The new limit meant that new post-fork blocks of 1 MB would not be rejected by pre-fork blocks which had no limit, but if miners attempted to add a 2 MB block (which would have been accepted pre-fork), that block would be rejected after the 2010 soft fork because it violated the 1 MB limit set by the soft fork.

After a soft fork, miners must upgrade to the new post-fork software. Else, their old software could create blocks that violate the rules of the soft fork and would be rejected by the post-fork software, a costly waste of computing power with no chance of earning a block reward.

Hard fork

A hard fork is not backwards compatible, meaning operations that occur on the new chain cannot occur on the old chain. For example, assume a chain had a maximum block size of 1 MB, and that chain executed a hard fork increasing the maximum block size to 4 MB. After the fork, a 2 MB block would be accepted by the new post-fork chain, but that 2 MB block would be rejected by the pre-fork chain because it exceeded the 1 MB maximum block size.

Chain splits

> *What is good among one people is an abomination with others.*
> —Chinua Achebe, *Things Fall Apart*

A chain split occurs when there are two or more competing versions of a blockchain after a fork. Chain splits can be caused by either a hard or a soft fork. The chart below depicts a chain split.

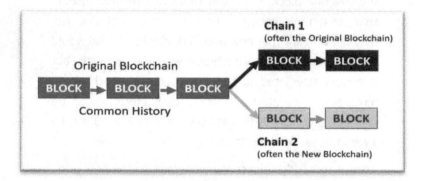

As seen above, both chains will have the same pre-fork history, but will have new and competing blockchains post-fork. To cause a chain to split, each side must have enough economic and computing power to continue to operate its preferred version of the blockchain. Generally, chain splits revolve around contentious technology proposals, often with each side believing that, over time, its side (the "right" side) will win and the other side (the "wrong" side) will fail.

There have been a number of Bitcoin-related hard forks, but two of the most significant were the August 2017 hard fork that created Bitcoin Cash, and the November 2018 Bitcoin Cash split that created Bitcoin ABC and Bitcoin SV described below.

The evolution of Bitcoin Cash forks. © AM

Bitcoin Cash fork

In November 2018, after a very public debate, Bitcoin Cash executed a hard fork which resulted in two new coins being created: Bitcoin ABC and Bitcoin SV. During the battle to see which coin would become the "real" Bitcoin Cash, both factions (i) claimed to be the legitimate Bitcoin Cash, and (ii) sought to claim the symbol "BCH," which would indicate to the public a "winner" of the battle.

Much of the fight spilled out onto the public, and at the time, there were numerous media reports of threats, cross-chain sabotage, and retaliation. To engage in the battle, groups of miners (mining pools) diverted significant hashing power to their respective sides. Estimates suggest that the ABC and SV groups spent upwards of $700,000 per day seeking dominance for their respective sides.

One cause of the rift was block size: Bitcoin ABC (ABC was short for "Adjustable Blocksize Cap") wanted to maintain the BCH 32 MB block size,[17] while Bitcoin SV (SV was short for Satoshi's Vision) wanted to increase the block size to 128 MB. Because neither side could come to agreement, both sides used the hard fork to implement their desired block size.

Immediately before the hard fork, many crypto exchanges halted BCH trading, not only because of the uncertainty surrounding the chain split, but also because it was unclear whether, or which, post-fork split chain would be allowed to call itself "Bitcoin Cash." Over time, the ABC group appeared to have come out on top. Many exchanges now refer to Bitcoin ABC as simply Bitcoin Cash (BCH), but Bitcoin SV is still a viable chain. According to coinmarketcap.com, by market capitalization at the end of 2019, Bitcoin ABC (listed as Bitcoin Cash (BCH)) had a market cap of

---

[17] In May 2018, Bitcoin Cash increased its block size from 8 MB to 32 MB through a hard fork. That hard fork also allowed developers to build smart contracts on top of the Bitcoin Cash network.

approximately $4.9 billion, and Bitcoin SV had a market cap of approximately $2.9 billion.

Identity on the Blockchain[18]

Having and proving one's identity is integral to functioning in modern society. According to Article 8 of the United Nations Convention on the Rights of the Child, everyone has a right to an identity. However, over 1.1 billion people worldwide cannot claim ownership over their identities because they do not have the necessary documentation to prove their identities. Absent such proof, their ability to participate in society, to own property, vote, receive government services, open a bank account, or find full-time employment is limited or non-existent.

An individual's proof of identity often consists of the state-provided means to authenticate oneself. In the US, those include birth certificates, Social Security numbers, driver's licenses, and passports. All require holding and keeping a physical document that contains various forms of identity data. In many cases, when people need to prove their identity, turning over one of those documents means providing more information than the other side needs, which risks compromising the person's privacy and security. A digital ID, securely maintained on a public blockchain, could help eliminate that risk. However, a great deal of work is left to be done.

For example, imagine Bibi just turned twenty-one and wanted to buy a cold Pliny the Elder (a truly outstanding beer, unfortunately not available outside of the western US) at the local watering hole. When she walks in, the bartender asks to see her ID to make sure she is of legal drinking age. The bartender only needs one piece of information, her date of birth. But in reality, he does not even need that; he only needs an answer to the binary question of whether she is over twenty-one.

---

[18] Much of this section is based on a series of articles authored by Justine Humenansky, Blockchain at Berkeley consultant, and Blockgenic, published in Hacker Noon.

However, when she hands over her ID, she not only proves she is over 21, but also gives the bartender a trove of other personal information, including her full name, her address, her birthday, and her driver's license number. A trusted blockchain-based digital identity (blockchain ID) could allow Bibi to let the bartender know she is over twenty-one and keep the rest of her information private, protecting both her personal data and her safety.

A blockchain ID would provide additional benefits as well, including:

- giving individuals control over their private data, thereby eliminating the ability of others, including credit card companies, social media companies, and large search engine companies, from profiting from individuals' private data; and

- making large-scale data theft more difficult, as large companies would no longer hold users' data, making them less attractive honeypots for hackers.

A blockchain ID would be especially valuable to two at-risk populations:

Refugees. Estimates are that over twenty million refugees no longer have access to their legal identities. The United Nations Human Rights Commission is exploring how a blockchain ID could help refugees prove their identities, share their identities with others for working or assistance purposes, and potentially store wealth as they flee their home countries.

The Homeless. Many homeless people have difficulty maintaining their possessions, including identification documents. A blockchain ID would not only allow them to prove their identities, but also allow service providers to better assist them in meeting their social and welfare needs.

Blockchain ID: Easier said than done

Creating a blockchain ID faces many obstacles before it can be implemented. Among the problems are:

What data will be used?

In order to create a blockchain ID, there needs to be some consensus regarding what types of data should be used to verify a person's identity. Three potential types of data are as follows:

1) *Something the person knows:* passwords, code phrases, unique information. One problem with this type of data is that it can be forgotten; also, it becomes useless when a person is incapacitated or cannot communicate.

2) *Something the person has:* a physical thing, such as a card or a key. Often, this type of data is coupled with some other type of data. For example, a debit card and a PIN is a combination of something a person has and something a person knows. An obvious problem with this type of data is that it can be lost or stolen.

3) *Something the person is:* biometric information, like fingerprints, facial recognition, retinal scans, etc. One problem with this type of data is that it requires at least one party to have a device that can read and verify the data.

How is the ID maintained?

A blockchain ID would likely be maintained on a mobile phone, which could be lost, stolen, or hacked. Alternatively, a blockchain ID could be something that could not be lost, which means it would need to be "something the person is," from above. Some forms are already in existence (fingerprints, retinal scans, biometric data), and others, like implanted chips, are the fodder for science fiction (though they are currently used in some places today).

Who maintains the data?

The issuance and storage of identity data are generally under the control of a government. Today, IDs are physical documents issued and validated by governments. If there were a blockchain ID created by a government, that same government would have the power to erase the ID, particularly for its more troublesome citizens. That risk may not seem particularly high in countries that purport to protect their citizens' freedom, but that is not the case in authoritarian countries or countries that openly repress dissent.

How are the data coordinated across the globe?

It is unlikely all the world's governments would agree on one system for a blockchain ID. As a result, a system of coordination would be needed, and some organization would need to maintain that system.

Although there are many to-be-solved problems regarding a blockchain ID, Estonia offers a useful model for implementing and operating such a system.

Estonia's e-Identity (eID) program[19]

Estonia has the most advanced digital ID system in the world and provides a model for how a blockchain ID could be implemented.

---

[19] Much of this section is based on a series of articles authored by Matt Reynolds, in *Wired* magazine, and Justine Humenansky, Blockchain at Berkeley consultant.

Wired magazine named Estonia "the most advanced digital society in the world," based, in part, on its eID program.

The eID program allows Estonians to pay taxes, vote online, as well as access public, financial, and medical services. Under the eID program, all citizens receive a secure digital ID card powered by a blockchain-like infrastructure that utilizes 2,048-bit public and private key encryption. All eID operations are PIN protected, and in the last few years, the eID program added QR codes and a Smart-ID mobile application to provide greater security. The eID program, like public blockchains, runs on open-source software.

The databases supporting the government's eID-accessed services are housed on over nine-hundred databases distributed across the country, a measure to make cyberattacks more difficult and, in the event of a successful attack, less costly to correct. That measure was taken based on past successful Russian cyberattacks, which shut down an Estonian bank and disrupted Estonian government services for over a month. The eID program, and the Estonian government's focus on cybersecurity, has made it more difficult for Russia to meddle in Estonia's election, as Russia did both in supporting Brexit in the United Kingdom (UK) and helping elect the successor to President Barack Obama in the United States.

PART II

The Crypto Value Proposition

Money as Technology

Bitcoin and other crypto derive their value from the utility they provide. That utility, often filling an unmet need, increasing efficiency, or decreasing transaction costs, explains why in just a little over eleven years, there are over five thousand cryptos, with a collective market cap of over $200 billion.

Identifying the value proposition for all types of crypto projects is obviously beyond the scope of this or any book. However, to date the most promising use case for crypto is as a new form of money. This chapter examines that value proposition by analyzing bitcoin and stablecoins, the most used and valuable money-type crypto projects.

To explain the value proposition for crypto as money, it is important to first provide:

1) a brief history of money as a form of technology;

2) a description of the historical use of gold both as a form of money and as collateral for money; and

3)   an examination of governments' role in the regulation of money over the last century.

That background lays the foundation for understanding crypto's value proposition.

Money is one of civilization's earliest and most important technological inventions, and serves three purposes: a medium of exchange, a store of value, and a unit of account.

<u>Medium of Exchange[1]</u>

Money eliminates the need for transactions based solely on the barter system, which requires a coincidence of wants between parties. The figures and examples below explain how money improves and simplifies transactions.

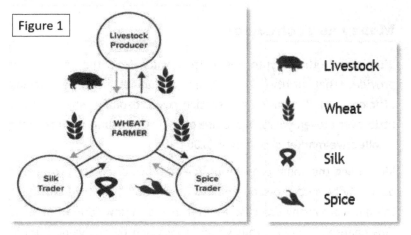

Figure 1 above shows a pure barter system with four participants: a wheat farmer, a livestock producer, a silk trader, and a spice trader, each of whom wants to sell items in a marketplace. This barter system is inefficient because the wants of the participants may not coincide. The livestock producer may be willing to trade for wheat to feed the livestock, but the wheat farmer may not have a direct,

---

[1]   This section borrows from an analysis by Matthew Beck, CFA, of Grayscale Investments, entitled, *Bitcoin & the Rise of Digital Gold.*

immediate use for livestock. Moreover, the wheat farmer may not know or appreciate the true value of livestock, due to insufficient market knowledge or limited access to trading partners. As a result, the wheat farmer and livestock producer may be unwilling to trade, though both would be better off if they could obtain the true value of the respective assets.

Money solves the problem.

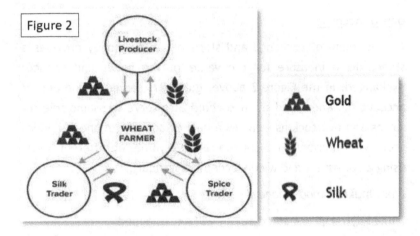

In Figure 2 above, the participants use money, in this case gold, to trade. Figure 2 demonstrates how trading with a form of money like gold improves upon the barter system by eliminating transactional inefficiencies. With the introduction of money, the wheat farmer will sell wheat to the livestock producer for gold and can use that gold to purchase anything she wants, including silk and spices. All participants are better off with the introduction of money, because money allows them to easily convert their goods into a universally accepted medium of exchange.

Store of Value

In order to serve as a medium of exchange, money must either provide a stable value over time or be expected to increase in value. A money's stability allows buyers and sellers to estimate, at the time of their transaction and into the near future, how much value is at stake. The more stable a money's value, the more willing users are to use it as a medium of exchange. Stable money provides security regarding the quantum of value that is, or will be, exchanged in transactions. Conversely, money expected to increase in value over time is less likely to be used as a medium of exchange, because people will tend to hold on to it to capture its expected future value.

<u>Unit of Account</u>

As a medium of exchange and store of value, money provides a standardized measure for the value of the goods and services exchanged. In the Figure 2 above, gold bars served as the unit of account for wheat and silk and could also serve the same role for spices and livestock as well. As a unit of account, money provides users with information about the relative values of different assets using a consistent and widely accepted standard.

What makes "good" money?

While anything considered money will act as a medium of exchange, a store of value, and a unit of account, those bare-minimum requirements do not address the effectiveness of a particular type of money. To be effective, a form of money generally must be:

> **Scarce:** supply needs to be limited in some way so that it maintains its value.

> **Verifiable:** there must be a means to test the money to ensure it is legitimate.

> **Durable:** money should not waste away, decay, or be easily destroyed.

> **Portable:** money should be easy to carry or transport.

> **Divisible:** money should be divisible into different-sized units.

Fungible: each specific unit of money (for example, US dollar bills) should be interchangeable with other units of the same type.

Recognizable: money should be easily identified and verified.

In addition to the above, "good" money should be resistant to counterfeiting and other schemes that could devalue it, like the one described in the box below.

Money Schemes using Coins

The first coins were minted using precious metals such as gold and silver, and were designed to have a uniform weight. However, soon after their introduction, people began scraping off small pieces from the edges of coins and melting those pieces together to create new counterfeit coins.

As more people scraped the edges, the coins got smaller and less valuable. To stop the practice, mints around the world began adding perpendicular grooves called reeds along the edges of coins. The reeds made it easy for anyone looking at the coin to see if the edges had been shaved off. The practice of adding reeds to coins continues today, as both the US quarter and dime have reeded edges.

Types of money that do not meet all those criteria may nevertheless be valuable. For example, gold serves all three of the money purposes, but is often difficult to transport, not easily divisible (without melting it), and hard to verify to the untrained eye. Despite those shortcomings, gold has served as the world's primary forms of money for thousands of years.

Gold as Money

Gold has been used for centuries both as money and as collateral backing other forms of money. Gold's value is derived from its unique physical chemical characteristics and its relative scarcity.

As an element, gold does not decay, serves as a good conductor of electricity, resists corrosion and oxidation, and as a metal with a relatively low melting point, can be easily shaped into various forms. In addition to those physical characteristics, the annual production of gold is small relative to its global supply. Those properties have driven the demand for gold throughout history, and led nations and individuals to commit unspeakable acts of cruelty to acquire it.

Stock-to-Flow Ratio

There are roughly 190,000 tons of gold in existence above ground today. However, throughout history, on average only about 1-to-3 percent of the then-existing supply of gold is mined per year. That low production coupled with strong demand explains a significant portion of gold's value proposition.

As an economic measure, gold's annual production relative to its existing supply is reflected by a metric called a stock-to-flow ratio, defined as the amount of an asset held in reserves (stock), divided by the amount produced every year (flow). Higher stock-to-flow ratios indicate that the total supply of an asset will not increase significantly year to year, thus increases in supply will be small relative to the total stock of the asset.

Gold has the highest stock-to-flow of any commodity asset. Current estimates indicate that gold has a stock-to-flow ratio of about 62, which represents the total amount of above-ground gold (roughly 190,000 tons), divided by the amount of gold produced annually (estimated to be a little over 3,000 tons). In contrast, silver has a stock-to-flow ratio of roughly 22, platinum has a stock-to-flow ratio of 0.4, and palladium has a stock-to-flow ratio of 1.1.

If all the gold mined throughout history were in one place, it would fit into a cube sixty-eight feet (twenty-one meters) on all sides, and would fill about four Olympic-sized swimming pools. At current valuations, all that gold is worth about $7.8 trillion.

Gold: The World's Money

For the past few thousand years or so, prior to the advent of paper money, gold served as the primary world money. Gold was mined in Nubia (modern day Sudan and Egypt) from as far back as 4000 BCE. At first, gold was traded by weight and served as a unit of account for payment.

Around 550 BCE, the first gold coins were minted using electrum, a natural alloy of gold and silver found in modern-day western Turkey. Gold continued to be used as money through the centuries, and the thirst for gold led many Europeans to plunder both Africa and the Americas without regard for the human costs of their actions. Historical records indicate that the Portuguese first enslaved Africans to mine gold as far back as 1470, and European slavers continued to use enslaved Africans to mine gold well into the 19th century.

Towards the end of the 17th century, European banks and governments began to introduce paper money exchangeable into gold. Because gold backed so many forms of money around the globe, it became the *de facto* world reserve currency.

Paper Money

Paper money was first created by the Chinese during the Tang

Tang Dynasty
618 – 907

Dynasty, well before paper money was used in Europe. During his service to the Mongol Khan Kublai in the late 1200s, Marco Polo noted the use of paper money throughout what is now modern-day China.

Gold's use as a reserve currency lasted until the latter half of the 20th century, when most governments began to issue fiat money that was not backed by anything other than the full faith and credit of the government.

Today, the US dollar has replaced gold and serves as the world's primary reserve currency. At the end of 2019, US dollars accounted for roughly 62 percent of all known central bank foreign exchange reserves, 47 percent of global payments, as well as 88 percent of foreign exchange trading. Understanding how the dollar replaced gold as the world's reserve currency requires an understanding of the 1944 Bretton Woods agreement.

Bretton Woods: The Short Version

Before the 1944 Bretton Woods agreement, most world currencies were on a gold standard, meaning those currencies were exchangeable into gold on demand. In effect, those local currencies were IOUs from the governments that issued them, backed by a promise to deliver gold when requested. That promise meant that a government could not, in theory, print more paper currency at will; it could only print as much currency as it held in gold reserves.

I can't be overdrawn; I still have more checks!
—Old Joke

However, limits on printing money are like limits on writing checks: although it is imprudent to write checks in amounts greater than held in a bank account, people do it all the time. The same has been true for governments.

During World War I, many countries realized that they needed more money to finance their war efforts than they had in gold reserves, and abandoned the gold standard by printing more currency than they held in gold reserves. Those actions increased the money supply. However, the increase in money supply coupled with the decrease in the production and supply of goods brought on by the war efforts led to inflation.

After the war, many countries returned to the gold standard. However, a little over a decade after the end of World War I, the 1929 stock market crash and Great Depression created a world financial crisis. That crisis prompted many individuals and speculators to try to acquire gold, viewing it as a store of value during a difficult financial period. As a result, both the demand for, and the price of, gold increased dramatically.

Ten years after the Great Depression, World War II erupted, which put increased stress on the world's financial system, and those financial stresses continued throughout the war. Toward the end of World War II in 1944, the 44 Allied World War II nations gathered in Bretton Woods, New Hampshire, to address the world financial crisis. That gathering established the international monetary policy framework called the Bretton Woods system.

The goal of Bretton Woods was to provide a framework of monetary and financial stability to foster economic growth and international trade. That framework was responsible for the International Monetary Fund and the World Bank, and lasted until the early 1970s.

As part of the Bretton Woods system, the Allied Nations agreed to peg their exchange rates to the US dollar, meaning their currencies would be exchangeable into a set amount of US dollars. In exchange, the United States agreed to convert dollars into gold on demand.

When the Bretton Woods system was implemented, the United States held approximately 75 percent of the world's gold supply. Interestingly though, US citizens were prohibited from owning gold at the time. In 1933, President Franklin Delano Roosevelt issued Executive Order 6102, making it illegal for US citizens to own gold, either in coins or in bars. The order generally required all citizens to hand over their gold to the US government for $20.67 per ounce, or face a ten-year prison sentence and a fine of twice the amount of gold not surrendered. The criminal prohibition was not lifted until 1974.

As part of the Bretton Woods system, world governments agreed to direct their central banks to buy or sell their currencies on world foreign exchange markets to strengthen or weaken those currencies in order to maintain the pegged exchange rates. For example, if a country's currency became weak (see box below for an explanation of strong and weak currencies) relative to the dollar, the country's central bank could purchase its currency in foreign exchange markets to reduce supply and raise the price of its currency relative to the dollar. Alternatively, if a foreign currency strengthened relative to the dollar, the central bank could print more currency, thereby increasing the country's money supply and lowering the currency's price relative to the dollar.

"Strong" and "weak" currencies

The best way to explain strong or weak currencies is with an example. Assume Country X has a currency, the "ZEX," that is pegged ten to one to the dollar, meaning 10 ZEX = $1.

If country X's currency value became weak compared to the dollar, it would mean that more than 10 ZEX would be needed to buy one dollar. As a result:

- Country X products would be cheaper to US consumers, giving US consumers more purchasing power, and

- Country X exports to the US, and US imports from Country X, would likely increase.

Alternatively, if the ZEX strengthened relative to the dollar, it would take less than 10 ZEX to purchase one dollar. As a result,

- US products would be cheaper to Country X consumers, giving Country X consumers more purchasing power, and

- Country X imports from the US, and US exports to Country X, would likely increase.

Conflicts over the relative strength of currencies has often led to trade wars and tariffs on imported goods. Most economists would agree that trade wars tend to be counterproductive for citizens of all countries engaged in them. Nevertheless, politicians can use trade wars to reward or protect a certain industry or group, at the expense of the citizenry as a whole.

The Bretton Woods system effectively ended on August 15, 1971, when the United States unilaterally abandoned the gold standard.

Why did the United States abandon the gold standard?

The complete answer is a complicated mix of historical facts and bad fiscal and monetary policy, but the simple explanation is the US did not have enough gold in reserve to meet its growing obligations to deliver gold. That lack of gold reserves led President Nixon to cause the US to renege on its promise to back the dollar with gold.

The facts below, in chronological order, help explain how the US got into that position:

- In 1960, the US held $19.4 billion in gold reserves, and there were roughly $18.7 billion in dollars held outside the US.

- During the 1960s and early 1970s, US citizens purchased increasingly more imported goods using dollars, but did not sell enough domestically produced goods overseas to bring those dollars back to the US. That created a balance of payments deficit with foreign governments.

- Also during the 1960s and early 1970s, the Soviet Union began producing significant amounts of oil and selling that oil for dollars, thereby accumulating dollars. Because of Cold War tensions, the Soviets deposited their dollars in European banks, creating what became known as eurodollars. The term "eurodollars" now generally refers to all US dollar deposits held overseas.

- As more eurodollars were held overseas, the balance of payments deficit grew, and foreign governments lost confidence in the US's Bretton Woods promise to exchange gold for dollars.

- By 1970, eurodollar holdings exceeded $45 billion, while US gold reserves were only worth approximately $14.5 billion.

- By the early 1970s, the Nixon government was engaged in the latter stages of an expensive war with Vietnam. Those expense included both the costs of the war and the economic aid to the Saigon regime.

Most estimates indicate that the war cost $168 billion (about $1 trillion in today's dollars).

- By early-to-mid 1971, the US inflation rate had risen to 5 percent, and unemployment had risen to over 6 percent. High inflation coupled with stagnant economic growth and high unemployment is called stagflation. Stagflation in the US caused, among a host of other domestic problems, overseas and eurodollar deposits to lose value.

Based on the facts listed above, many world banks and governments began redeeming their dollar holdings for gold. In response to both the stagflation and the rising number of requests to exchange dollars for gold, Nixon issued an executive order on August 15, 1971 to (1) freeze all prices and wages for 90 days, and (2) stop the Federal Reserve from redeeming dollars for gold. The price controls temporarily reduced inflation, but within three years inflation rose to double-digit levels and persisted through the 1970s.

When Nixon abandoned the gold standard, it marked the first time in modern history that paper money was not at least nominally backed by some asset, and introduced the world to fiat currencies— currencies backed only by confidence in a government. In theory, all fiat currencies had a value relative to other fiat currencies, but those values were not linked, directly or indirectly, to any particular asset. However, the reality was a bit different.

Birth of the Petrodollar

The Secret Agreement to Strengthen the Dollar

With the end of Bretton Woods and the gold standard, a new system was needed for the US to maintain the dollar's status as the world's reserve currency. Enter the petrodollar.[2]

Shortly after the US abandoned the gold standard in 1971, the price of gold skyrocketed and the value of the US dollar weakened substantially. As a result, many existing contracts to purchase and sell oil that were priced in dollars became far less valuable. Then in October 1973, Arab members of Organization of the Petroleum Exporting Countries (OPEC) increased oil prices by over 70 percent and placed an embargo on exports to the US and other allies of Israel.

The OPEC increase in the oil prices was in response to the US siding with Israel in the "Yom Kippur" or "Ramadan War," after a coalition of Arab states led by Egypt and Syria launched an attack against Israeli positions on Yom Kippur, a Jewish holy day, and during Ramadan, a month of fasting in Islam.

The war that ensued lasted less than three weeks, but the embargo had the effect of increasing US oil prices roughly 400 percent over the next six months, contributing to a US stock market collapse, and bringing on the 1973 gas crisis, which forced US motorists to wait in long lines to get gas. That embargo coupled with the costs of the Vietnam War and US government policies (including wage and price controls) were significant contributors to the recessions in the 1970s.

---

[2]   Details of the creation of the petrodollar agreement were first widely reported by Andrea Wong in a May 2016 story in Bloomberg entitled, *The Untold Story Behind Saudi Arabia's 41-Year U.S. Debt Secret*.

The embargo lasted until 1974 when the Nixon administration entered into a series of secret military and economic agreements with the family that controlled Saudi Arabia to standardize oil contracts in US dollars. Those agreements had the effect of forcing world oil buyers to buy oil in US dollar terms, which allowed oil to replace gold as the *de facto* asset backing the dollar. In return, the Saudis agreed to invest those dollars back into US debt, allowing the US to more easily finance its spending. That system became known as the petrodollar.

By 1975, all OPEC nations agreed to price their oil exclusively in US dollars, mostly in exchange for weapons and military protection. Because oil is the world's most important commodity, the petrodollar helped strengthen the dollar and cemented its position as the world's reserve currency.

Economic and Fiscal Policy of the Petrodollar

The petrodollar system has significant benefits for the United States and oil-producing countries. For the US, it increased demand for US dollars around the globe, because dollars are needed to purchase oil. That increased demand strengthens the dollar and produces a surfeit of dollars, at little or no cost, for oil-producing countries, many of which are governed by regimes claiming to be royal or by other generally autocratic and undemocratic regimes.

The oil-producing countries that benefit from the petrodollar system often invest those surplus dollars in US government debt instruments, increasing demand for US-dollar-denominated debt. That increased demand helps keep interest rates low on US debt, and generally speaking, those low US interest rates encourage spending and investment in the US.

Although the petrodollar system benefits both the US and the OPEC nations, those benefits do not extend to other nations whose monetary and fiscal policies (see box below) cannot take advantage of the petrodollar system.

Monetary and Fiscal Policy

Monetary policy refers to how central banks manage their country's money supply, generally with four primary objectives:

1) managing inflation;

2) reducing unemployment;

3) maintaining low, but sustainable, interest rates; and

4) promoting growth.

Governments control the money supply by printing and distributing the local currency or by taking that currency out of circulation. By adding too much money, they can create run-away hyperinflation and destroy their economy. By not creating enough, they could, according to theories espoused by British economist John Maynard Keynes, stifle growth. But by adding or subtracting the "Goldilocks" amount of money—not too little, not too much—Keynesian theory posits that central banks can both stimulate the economy and maintain economic stability.

Fiscal policy, which is related to monetary policy, refers to the use of government spending and taxing policies to influence economic conditions. Much modern fiscal policy is also based, in part, on Keynes' theory that governments can stabilize the business cycle and regulate economic output by adjusting their monetary policies.

The primary fiscal policy tools available are:

- raising taxes (always unpopular);

- cutting spending (similarly unpopular);

> - borrowing money (works in the short-term, but absent economic growth, will eventually require raising taxes or cutting spending to pay the money back); or
>
> - printing money (which could lead to inflation, hurting all citizens because the money in circulation loses its buying power).

The petrodollar system provides flexibility for the US and oil-producing countries to implement fiscal policies because, in simple terms, there is more money available to solve problems. For the US, petrodollars give the US government far more flexibility than other countries to maintain continual deficits and an ever-growing national debt without adverse fiscal and monetary consequences.

The oil-producing petrodollar countries benefit both from the stable dollars they earn from their natural resources and the willingness of the US government to protect those resources and the governments that control them. Some assert that the willingness of the US to (i) provide military support to "friendly" OPEC nations like Saudi Arabia and Kuwait, and (ii) punish "unfriendly" oil producing nations like pre-invasion Iraq and Iran is based, at least in part, on the US's interest in protecting the dollar's sovereignty.[3]

To underscore that second assertion, many point to the state of affairs in Iraq during the early 2000s:

- In 2000, after Iraq threatened to suspend all oil exports (then about 5 percent of the world's supply), the United Nations (UN) gave Iraq, under its then-leader Saddam Hussein, permission to sell oil for euros instead of dollars.

---

[3] This book is not intended to support or refute that contention, but merely to present it because of its widespread belief.

- Over the next two-and-a-half years, the euro strengthened against the dollar. In October 2000, when the UN approved Iraq's request, the euro/dollar exchange rate was around 0.84 EUR for 1 US$. By early March 2003 (immediately before the invasion), the euro had appreciated over 43 percent to around 1.07 EUR = 1 US$.

- In 2003, the US invaded Iraq. The administration of President George W. Bush claimed the invasion was justified because Hussein had acquired a secret cache of weapons of mass destruction (WMDs). In the 17 years after the invasion, the secret cache of WMDs has yet to be discovered.

- After forces allied to the US regained control of the Iraqi oil fields, Iraqi oil contracts were again traded in US dollars.

The Weaponization of the Dollar

The petrodollar system gives the US outsized significance in world financial policy.[4] US politicians have the ability to use the power of the dollar to extend the reach of US law and policy to other countries. In the post-Obama administration, numerous attempts to weaponize the power of the dollar have been reported, including the 2018 prohibition on Iran using SWIFT (see box below).

Iran was first banned from SWIFT by the Obama administration in 2012, resulting in a decrease in Iran's oil exports from around 2.5 million barrels in 2011 to around one million barrels in 2014. However, after the US, Iran, and a coalition of world governments and all five permanent members of the UN Security Council agreed

---

[4]   See Jeffrey Frankel, *How a Weaponized dollar Could Backfire*, Harvard Kennedy School Belfer Center for Science and International Affairs (Oct. 28, 2019).

to the 2015 Joint Comprehensive Plan of Action (the Iran nuclear deal), the SWIFT ban was lifted, and Iranian oil exports increased.

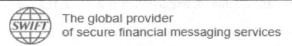
The global provider
of secure financial messaging services

SWIFT is the Belgium-based Society for Worldwide Interbank Financial Communications. SWIFT operates as a global collective that connects over 11,000 banks, financial institutions, and corporations in over 200 countries and territories across the globe. SWIFT allows participants to securely send, receive, and track information about financial transactions. Countries who do not participate, or are barred from SWIFT have limited means to make or receive international payments.

On May 8, 2018, the US unilaterally abandoned the Iran nuclear deal. Soon thereafter, the US administration began pressuring SWIFT to ban Iranian banks. On November 5, 2018, SWIFT capitulated, commenting that the ban was "regrettable," but necessary to avoid US sanctions and maintain the stability of the international banking system.

World frustration at the unilateral US action was evident, and China, Europe, and Russia took steps to counteract the US action, including:

- China signed a 25-year oil supply deal directly with Iran, allowing China to pay for oil using the Chinese yuan, thereby bypassing the petrodollar system altogether. The deal is expected to inject the equivalent of about $280 billion into Iran.

- The governments of France, Germany, and the UK developed INSTEX in 2019 as a mechanism to facilitate non-US dollar and non-SWIFT transactions to avoid US sanctions. INSTEX allows European businesses to trade with Iran without SWIFT. In November 2019, Belgium, Denmark, the Netherlands, Finland, and Sweden joined INSTEX.

- Russia agreed to bypass the SWIFT network by linking its banking system directly to Iran's.

Collectively, those actions signal a growing effort to limit both the benefits of the petrodollar and the ability of US politicians to weaponize the dollar.

Venezuela: A Case Study of What Can Go Wrong

The petrodollar system coupled with poor economic and fiscal policies can negatively affect citizens of a country. Post-2014 Venezuela serves as a prime example.

Before 2014, the Venezuelan economy was relatively prosperous, as the revenues from oil exports allowed Venezuela's long-serving president, Hugo Chavez, and his successor, Nicolas Maduro, to fund the government and support many popular social programs. That was possible because over 90 percent of the country's export earnings came from oil, and from 1999 to 2014, oil prices rose from $25 to over $160 per barrel and generally hovered between $100 and $125 per barrel.

Starting around 2014, a few things happened that caused the price of oil to drop: OPEC members produced more oil, the US began to produce more oil through hydraulic fracturing (fracking), and China experienced slowing economic growth. In other words, oil supply increased and demand decreased. An economics degree is not needed to understand what happens when supply increases and demand decreases: prices drop. From June 2014 to February 2016, oil prices dropped from a peak of $115 to $35 per barrel.

When the price of oil dropped, so did the demand for the Venezuelan currency, the bolívar. That caused the demand for, and the value of, the bolívar to fall precipitously relative to other world currencies.

Prior to the decline in oil prices, in January 2014 the Venezuelan bolívar to US dollar exchange rate was seventy to one, meaning 70 bolívars was exchangeable into $1. After the decline, by January 2016 that exchange rate was almost one thousand to one, or 1,000 bolívars for $1. As the value of the bolívar fell, the cost of imported goods for Venezuelans rose, and the Venezuelan economy went into crisis.

Soon after Maduro took over in 2013 after Chavez's death, Maduro had to determine how his government would respond to decreased demand for Venezuelan bolívars and low oil prices. His primary response was to print more bolívars, which first caused inflation, and eventually led to hyperinflation (see box below).

Hyperinflation and governments

Hyperinflation is very high and typically accelerating inflation which erodes the value of the local currency. The highest reported inflation rate in the last hundred years happened in Hungary in 1946, where the *daily* inflation rate was over 207 percent, and prices doubled roughly every 15.6 hours. In 2008, Zimbabwe experienced hyperinflation, and the daily inflation rate reached 98 percent, meaning prices doubled every 24.7 hours. During periods of hyperinflation, people often minimize their holdings in the local currency and, if possible, switch to more stable assets (like gold or cattle) or currencies (like the US dollar and, increasingly, crypto).

In 2014, Venezuela's inflation rate was 69 percent, then the highest in the world. By 2016, the inflation rate was between 800 percent and 4,000 percent.

In 2018, one of Maduro's responses to Venezuela's hyperinflation was to institute a 1,000-to-1 revaluation of the currency, changing the country's official currency from the "Bolívar fuerte" (the old bolívar) to the "Bolívar soberano," (the new bolívar), and making 1,000 units of the old Bolívar fuerte equal to 1 unit of the new Bolívar soberano. In US dollar terms, that would be equivalent to the US government forcing all citizens to turn over all their hundred-dollar bills and exchange them for newly-minted dimes.

The 2018 currency revaluation was a disaster. By May 2019, Venezuela's annual rate of inflation was over 815,000 percent (that is not a typo). Venezuela's economic crisis prompted over three million people to leave the country for neighboring Colombia and elsewhere. Many of those remaining stopped accepting and using the new bolívar, and instead sought to exchange their bolívars into US dollars, a far better store of value.

One of Venezuela's long-standing fiscal policies also exacerbated the crisis. Since 2003, Venezuela has had strict currency controls, limiting citizens' ability to exchange bolívars into other currencies. The government also set an official exchange rate that overvalued the bolívar compared to the dollar. The market response to those currency controls and exchange rate policies was the growth of an illegal market for dollars, as Venezuelans sought to buy dollars from the government and sell them in the illegal market for a profit.

That policy did little-to-nothing to help alleviate the effects of hyperinflation, but did create a new industry that has cost the government billions: currency tourism (see box below).

Currency Tourists and Favored Exchange Rates

Although there were strict limits on Venezuelan citizens' ability to exchange bolívars into dollars, there was an exception for citizens traveling internationally who had purchased a plane

---

ticket. Those citizens could exchange bolívars for dollars at the official rate of 6.3 bolívars for $1, with a limit of $3,000. However, the (illegal) market rate at the time was 45 bolívars for $1.

What many citizens did was exchange 18,900 bolívars for $3,000 (the limit) with the government, then turn around and sell those $3,000 for 135,000 bolívars in the illegal market, a 714 percent return. Those citizens often never actually traveled overseas and viewed the plane ticket as a cost of the transaction.

The Venezuelan government also gave favored individuals and industries access to preferred exchange rates. At one point in 2018, those in the favored group could exchange bolívars for dollars at a 10-to-1 rate, at a time when the official government rate was 3,345 to 1, and the illegal market rate was as high as 3.6 million to 1 (pre-revaluation). Former Venezuelan government officials and economists estimate that between $41 billion and $300 billion in state revenues were lost due to these types of foreign exchange machinations.

What does this have to do with Bitcoin?

A lot. Understanding government's role in the value of money is critical to explaining the attraction of bitcoin, a largely government-proof asset. Bitcoin's value is based, in large part, on (i) its similarities and improvements to gold as a form of money, and (ii) the inability of governments to control or manipulate it as part of their fiscal or monetary policies.

Bitcoin: Digital Gold

While gold has historically played a central role as a transactional currency, the world we live in today is digital. As the first widely-available native digital currency, bitcoin has the potential to displace, or at least compete with, gold as a store of value in a digital world. That's because in a digital global economy, bitcoin outperforms gold on many of the qualities that has made gold valuable:

> **Scarcity.** Like gold, bitcoins are scarce assets. Hard coded in the Bitcoin protocol is a strict 21 million supply, and no counterfeit bitcoins have ever been produced in its ten-plus year history. At the end of 2019, approximately 18.1 million of those 21 million bitcoins have been issued, and all 21 million will be issued by 2040. Current estimates are that between 2.8 and 3.8 million or so have been lost by users, meaning those users somehow lost the private keys to their bitcoins. For example, CNBC reported that James Howells, an English IT worker, threw away a hard drive containing 7,500 bitcoins in a local landfill.

> **Verifiability.** Bitcoins are unique cryptographic assets that are directly verifiable on the Bitcoin blockchain, in real time, from anywhere in the world. Unlike gold, it is not necessary to have bitcoins in any particular place to determine their authenticity. All that is needed is an internet connection.

> **Durability.** Bitcoins reside on an open-source network maintained by a global base of users. The open-source nature of the Bitcoin protocol has made the network incredibly durable to threats, eliminating single points of failure and allowing for continuous adaptation and improvement.

Portability. As native digital asses, bitcoins exist in cyberspace. With the simplest of mobile devices, the 4.7 billion global mobile phone users with an internet connection can already carry, send, spend, and receive bitcoins. In addition, technological developments may eliminate the need for an internet connection. For example, Blockstream and goTenna are developing technologies to complete bitcoin transactions via geosynchronous satellites and mesh networks, which will allow phones to connect directly with one another. Those technologies would give those without direct internet connections the ability to transact on the Bitcoin network, and frustrate any government's attempts to limit internet accessibility in order to prevent its citizens from using bitcoin.

Divisibility. All bitcoins are divisible into one hundred million units, called satoshis. Each satoshi (sometimes shortened to sat or sats) are worth 0.00000001 BTC. This allows Bitcoin to facilitate transactions of any size, as 1 satoshi is equal to $0.0001, or one hundredth of a penny (at the January 2020 price of $10,000 per BTC). The divisibility of sats makes it easier for individuals to collect them into a more sizable position, referred to generally as "stacking sats."

Fungibility. All bitcoins are, for the most part, interchangeable. The "for the most part" qualifier is included because chain analytics (discussed below) and recent regulations (discussed in Part III) make it possible to trace certain transactions to users. With the ability to track transactions and users, it may be possible to identify a certain individual's holdings, and if that individual has run afoul of a government, that government may identify that user's bitcoin as "tainted," and penalize individuals who accept tainted coins.

Recognizable. Despite its short history, the Bitcoin network has achieved global awareness and bitcoin transactions are possible in the majority of countries around the world.

Stock-to-flow ratios

A strong driver of bitcoin's value is its stock-to-flow ratio. As noted earlier, gold has a stock-to-flow ratio of around 62. At the end of 2019, bitcoin's stock-to-flow ratio was around 27.5, calculated by dividing the 18.1 million bitcoins in circulation (ignoring lost coins) by the 657,000 Bitcoins mined annually (12.5 bitcoins per block × 144 blocks per day × 365 days).

The market value of those bitcoins, at a price of $10,000 per BTC (the January 2020 price), is about $181 billion, or around 2.3 percent of the $7.8 trillion value of gold. Although a small percentage, bitcoin gained that value in just over ten years, while gold has accumulated its value over at least six thousand years.

While gold's stock-to-flow ratio has been relatively constant throughout history, bitcoin's stock-to-flow ratio is programmed to increase. The Bitcoin block reward is reduced by half every 210,000 blocks—roughly every four years. That reduction in the block reward is called a halvening.

A halvening occurred in May 2020 which decreased the block reward from 12.5 to 6.25 bitcoins per block, thereby reducing the number of bitcoins mined annually to roughly 328,500. That May 2020 halvening doubled bitcoin's stock-to-flow ratio to around 55, just below gold's stock-to-flow ratio of 62. By 2025, the estimated date of the next halvening, the stock-to-flow ratio will again double. At that point, unless gold miners stop finding gold to mine, bitcoin will have the highest stock-to-flow ratio of any commodity asset.

Various models have been created linking bitcoin's price using stock-to-flow ratios. Those models, by and large, show that bitcoin's price correlates well with what would be expected using a stock-to-flow model. One of the most discussed models, distributed on Medium by PlanB, shows a 99.7% correlation coefficient (a statistical measure of how well the model fits the actual data), and predicts a bitcoin price of $288,000 sometime in or before 2024.[5] An earlier, less sophisticated version of PlanB's model predicted a bitcoin price of $55,000 sometime in or before 2024.

So, what is the true value proposition for Bitcoin?

That is anyone's guess. Many point to bitcoin's stock-to-flow ratio and other comparisons to, and improvements on, gold to explain bitcoin's value proposition. Some take that argument further, claiming that bitcoin's properties will eventually allow it to replace gold as a store of value asset. Those making that claim often cite the fact that gold's role as a store of value asset is based, at its core, on little more than people's belief in its value. As the argument goes, as more and more people believe in bitcoin, it will compete with and possibly supplant gold as a store of value asset.

Clearly, the ultimate value of bitcoin is a speculative proposition. However, there are metrics to forecast how much bitcoin *could* be worth in the future. As we are in the realm of speculation, one such metric assumes that sometime in the future, bitcoin and gold will be equally valuable. At January 2020 valuations (1 BTC = $10,000), bitcoin's market capitalization was roughly $181 billion and those four Olympic swimming pools of gold were worth $7.8 trillion, collectively making them both worth around $8 trillion. Holding that $8 trillion constant, if we assume some time in the future that $8 trillion is split equally between bitcoin and gold, then all 21 million

---

[5] See PlanB, *Bitcoin Stock-to-Flow Cross Asset Model*, Medium (Apr. 27, 2020).

bitcoins would be collectively worth $4 trillion, or $380,952 per bitcoin. More or less.

Bitcoin volatility

Throughout its short history, the price of bitcoin has been volatile. The chart below, courtesy of Coinbase, shows that the price of bitcoin from 2013 through January 2020, with a high price of over $20,000 and a low of below $100.

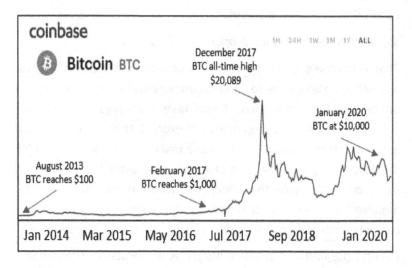

Bitcoin's volatility makes it impracticable for merchants or consumers to use it as a medium of exchange, because from day-to-day and week-to-week the value fluctuates. Nevertheless, that volatility and the long-term increases in value have caused many to treat bitcoin as an investment or speculative store of value asset.

The chart below shows the gross returns from investing $100 in bitcoin over time, from the start dates listed below through December 31, 2019, when bitcoin was valued at $7,199.53.

Investment returns of Bitcoin through December 31, 2019			
START DATE	BTC PRICE	Cumulative return %	Annualized return %***
January 1, 2011*	$0.30	2,426,135%	307%
January 1, 2012*	$5.27	145,640%	248%
January 1, 2013*	$13.30	53,721%	246%
January 1, 2014	$771.40	863%	146%
January 1, 2015	$314.25	2,198%	187%.
January 1, 2016	$443.34	1,548%	201%
January 1, 2017	$998.33	599%	191%
January 1, 2018**	$13,657	-49%	71%
January 1, 2019	$3,843	86%	186%

* Bitcoin was not regularly traded on exchanges until 2013, and pre-2014 price data are based on the CoinDesk Bitcoin Price Index, among other sources.

** Bitcoin reached its highest price, at just over $20,000, in December 2017.

*** An annualized total return is the return that would produce the same cumulative return if the return was compounded, and is the geometric average amount of money earned by an investment each year over a given time period.

Bitcoin and Governments

Another important value factor of bitcoin and other crypto is that they are largely immune from government intervention. Although governments can enact legislation making it more difficult for their citizens to hold or use bitcoin, it would be difficult for a government to implement a complete bitcoin ban. Even if banned, it would be difficult to enforce such a ban.

As a decentralized, borderless, and pseudonymous system accessible to anyone in the world with an internet connection, even the most repressive governments have limited power to stop their citizens from using bitcoin. Some have compared an attempt to outlaw or limit bitcoin to the failed war on drugs in the United States. That so-called war, started in the 1970s when Nixon stated that drug abuse was "public enemy number one," did little to change drug use; in fact, from 1973 to 1977, drug use in the United States doubled. Unfortunately, the war on drugs had far-reaching negative effects both for the US and other nations around the globe: it increased the prison population, disproportionately criminalized black and brown citizens despite the fact that there is no significant difference in drug use between minority and non-minority populations,[6] and led to tens of thousands of trafficking-related murders across the globe, particularly in Colombia and Mexico.

A government attempt to ban Bitcoin would make clear two things:

- the government is interested in restricting the freedom of its citizens; and

- bitcoin must be valuable, else why would the government want to ban it?

---

[6]   African Americans and whites use drugs at similar rates, but the imprisonment rate of African Americans for drug charges is almost 6 times that of whites. In addition, though African Americans and Hispanics make up approximately 32 percent of the US population, they comprised 56 percent of all incarcerated people in 2015.

Any government seeking to ban Bitcoin would also face many of the same challenges faced when outlawing other *malum prohibitum* items,[7] as was the case during Prohibition in the US, and is currently the case with respect to the disjointed federal and state recreational marijuana use laws.

At the end of 2019, the following countries had imposed some type of ban on Bitcoin:

- Afghanistan
- Algeria
- Bolivia
- Bangladesh
- Ecuador
- Iran
- Nepal
- Pakistan
- Saudi Arabia

Those countries, ruled by what few would consider freedom-loving governments, show little consistency in their bans. Some prohibit bitcoin ownership outright, while others prohibit bitcoin's use as a means of payment, and are permissive or at least agnostic regarding their citizens' rights to own and trade bitcoin.

---

[7] *Malum prohibitum* is a Latin phrase referring to things or actions that are unlawful not because they are necessarily bad or evil, but solely because a government has written laws making those things or actions unlawful. In contrast, *malum in se* refers to things or actions that are bad or evil in themselves. Non-government approved gambling is an example of something that is *malum prohibitum*, and stealing from a charity is an example of something that is *malum in se*.

Bitcoins as Money: Privacy and Pseudonymity

Crypto transactions are pseudonymous, meaning they are linked to publicly available digital addresses but not directly to an identity. Those public addresses are hashed versions of public keys, which are long strings of numbers that identify blockchain addresses. To enter into a transaction, a user needs both the public key and a private key known only to the user. The public/private key system allows individuals to engage in transactions without revealing their identities, despite the individuals' public keys being visible on the blockchain.

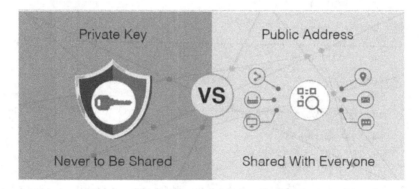

Graphic courtesy of bitira.com

Although crypto transactions are designed to be pseudonymous, because all transactions leave a digital trail, digital sleuths have created ways to link transactions through what is called chain analytics, which links publicly visible transactions to specific accounts, activities, wallets, and ultimately, individuals. One beneficial use of chain analytics has been by law enforcement agencies who have used chain analytics to successfully find and charge criminals. For example, on October 16, 2019, the Department of Justice (DOJ) issued the following press release, excerpted below:

The investigation resulted in leads sent to 38 countries and yielded

FOR IMMEDIATE RELEASE   Wednesday, October 16, 2019

South Korean National and Hundreds of Others Charged Worldwide in the Takedown of the Largest Darknet Child Pornography Website, Which was Funded by Bitcoin

Dozens of Minor Victims Who Were Being Actively Abused by the Users of the Site Rescued

According to the press release, the investigation led to the arrest of 337 subjects around the world and the rescue of at least 23 minor victims who were being abused by the website's users.

To find the criminals, DOJ and the IRS Criminal Investigation (IRS CI) used software developed by Chainalysis, a chain analytics company, to track the public keys of users of the website, and then linked those public keys to the accounts and individuals who used bitcoin to pay or receive funds related to the child pornography website. In addition to DOJ, other law enforcement agencies, such as Homeland Security, the Federal Bureau of Investigation (FBI), and the US Drug Enforcement Agency have used chain analytics to pursue terrorist organizations, organized crime, and drug traffickers.

Chain analytics is not only a tool of law enforcement. Chain analytics company CipherTrace announced in October 2018 that its platform allowed its private clients to trace over 87 percent of the transaction volume of the top 100 cryptos. Those clients include financial institutions seeking to comply with financial transactions rules, as well as private companies who wish to use chain analytics as part of their business models.

Privacy v. Security

Because chain analytics makes it easier to reduce the privacy associated with crypto, a number of services have evolved to defeat the effectiveness of chain analytics. Those services make it more difficult to link transactions to individual accounts or users. Those services expose the privacy/security tradeoff in crypto.

Coinjoins (sometimes called tumblers or mixers) are one method devised to defeat chain analytics. Coinjoins are services or applications that let users mix and exchange their coins with those of other users. After the coins are exchanged amongst users, sometimes multiple times, it is more difficult to determine and trace prior ownership of the coins, thus defeating chain analysis and preserving users' privacy.

Privacy coins offer another alternative to defeat chain analytics and maintain financial privacy. By and large, those coins obscure almost all transaction details on their blockchains, making it difficult or impossible to link transactions to users.

It is difficult to determine the most popular privacy coin (they are, after all, private), but most sources agree that Monero (XMR) is the most widely used privacy coin. Monero originally used what was called a CryptoNight proof of work protocol that obfuscated the blockchain's ledger of transactions, making it difficult or impossible to identify any transactional details. In October 2019, Monero switched to a new proof of work algorithm in order to increase the networks' security and decentralization. Monero implemented the change in consensus mechanism to ensure that mining on its network was not dominated by miners using more sophisticated and expensive ASIC chips in their computers.[8]

---

[8]   Because of the costs involved in mining with ASIC-powered machines, fewer users were able to mine XMR, making the network more centralized and less secure. The new consensus mechanism made it easier for computers using standard CPUs or GPUs to mine XMR, thereby reducing the advantages of ASIC chips.

It has been reported that Monero was the most popular crypto for AlphaBay transactions. Before being shut down in 2017, AlphaBay was the largest marketplace on the darknet (the part of the internet that uses custom software to ensure privacy), and was often used to facilitate criminal activities, from illegal file sharing to extortion and child pornography. Monero was also used by the WannaCry hackers, who, according to a September 2018 DOJ indictment, were a North Korean hacking and ransomware ring. According to the DOJ and FBI, the WannaCry hackers converted their criminal proceeds into Monero.

One popular privacy coin that has taken a more moderate approach to privacy is Zcash (ZEC), which offers users two transactional options: public and shielded. According to Zcash:

> *If a user opts to shield her funds, they are no longer visible on the blockchain. Once shielded, funds can be transferred using shielded transactions, which preserves the privacy of both the sender and the recipient. This facilitates compliance with regulations that mandate privacy for personal financial information, such as the Gramm-Leach-Bliley Act in the US, and the General Data Protection Regulation (GDPR) in the EU.*

In late 2019, it was announced that Zcash tokens would operate on the Ethereum blockchain, potentially allowing smart contracts to feature some of Zcash's privacy features.

Some regulators have taken public positions against privacy coins. In spring 2019, both French and Japanese regulators suggested banning privacy coins. The head of the Finance Committee of France's National Assembly, Eric Woerth, citing "fraud, tax evasion [and] money laundering," concerns, stated:

> *"It would also have been appropriate to propose a ban on the dissemination and trade in [cryptocurrencies built] to*

ensure complete anonymity by preventing any identification procedure by design. This is the case for a certain number of [cryptocurrencies] (Monero, PIVX, DeepOnion, Zcash. . .) whose purpose is to bypass any possibility of identifying the holders."[9]

In April 2018, Japanese financial regulators suggested a similar ban.

Is financial privacy important?

Many believe coinjoins and privacy coins are only useful for criminals. Others point out the myriad legitimate reasons to protect one's transactional privacy and believe coinjoins and privacy coins give individuals needed control over their financial sovereignty. Also, as surveillance becomes more ubiquitous by both businesses and governments, the ability to avoid leaving digital footprints whenever and wherever money is spent will become more important to maintain one's privacy.

> *"In an age in which businesses collect, analyze and sell our private information, it makes enormous sense to have legislation which protects the privacy of our financial transactions."*
> —Arnold Spencer, General Counsel for Coinsource and former Assistant U.S. Attorney in Texas

Balance is certainly needed in this area. Although anonymity may help criminals and terrorists evade government oversight, privacy and anonymity over financial matters is needed in order to maintain the freedoms, in the US at least, guaranteed by the Constitution.

---

[9]   See N° 1624, Assemblée Nationale, Rapport D'Information (Jan. 30, 2019).

Stablecoins

Stablecoins are crypto designed to maintain a stable value. Both stablecoins and other crypto like bitcoin represent a disruptive technology that has the potential to change the financial system. Unlike those other crypto, however, stablecoins provide the benefits of crypto—secure, transparent, decentralized, and fast payments—without price volatility.

Because of their price volatility, many crypto are ill-suited to serve as media of exchange. Instead, like gold, they are often held (hodled) as speculative store of value investments. The "hodling" of crypto exposed a need for crypto that could maintain a stable value and be used primarily as a medium of exchange.

Stacking Sats

In the Bitcoin community, a meme has developed around the continuous accumulation of satoshis (sats) to help hodlers acquire a larger position in bitcoin over time. It is unclear who created the term, but its popularity increased when it was adopted by crypto podcaster Matt Odell and recirculated with the Twitter handle #stackingsats.

Through the first half of 2019, over 225 stablecoin projects had been announced, and of those, roughly 60 were in operation. By April 2020, Tether was the most dominant stablecoin, with a market cap of roughly $6 billion and a daily trading volume of over $20 billion. Tether's market cap and trading volume are more than the combined amounts of Tether's top five competitors (TrueUSD, USD Coin, Paxos, Gemini, and DAI).

Stablecoins provide an effective and cost-efficient means for mobile payments. In the United States, where mobile payments are roughly 15 percent of all payments, the mobile payment market is dominated by companies like PayPal, Square Cash, and Venmo, which often charge transaction fees of 2.75 percent or more. Stablecoins transferred directly from consumers to businesses could eliminate those fees.

Stablecoins are also used as a temporary holding asset for crypto traders or businesses, eliminating the risk of holding unstable crypto. This use case evolved because many crypto exchanges, based on anti-money-laundering and other regulatory concerns, placed restrictions or limits on their customers' ability to exchange crypto into fiat currencies. Stablecoins thus provide a resting place for crypto owners to avoid volatility, and are often used to lock in crypto profits without trading into a fiat currency.

Stablecoins can also produce societal benefits, providing financial technology to populations without access to financial services, often referred to as the "unbanked." The World Bank estimates are that about three-quarters of the world's poorest individuals are unbanked, between 1.7 and 2 billion adults. However, according to the United Nations, 1.1 billion of the unbanked have access to mobile phones. Stablecoins offer the unbanked a greater opportunity to participate in the financial system, giving them access to a technology that allows them to store and accumulate wealth in an easily transportable and secure form.

Stablecoins also provide a stable form of money to people living in places with unstable currencies. In such cases, individuals can opt out of their local currencies and opt into stablecoins, thereby avoiding any instability or inflation in their local currencies. For example, during the hyperinflationary period in Venezuela, some citizens exchanged their bolívars into stablecoins, preserving their wealth and purchasing power and avoiding the effects of government-caused hyperinflation.

While such a system provides obvious benefits for citizens, the same is not true for governments of countries with unstable currencies. If citizens of those countries opt out of the local currency and use stablecoins, the demand for the government's fiat money will decrease. As that demand drops, so does the efficacy of printing more of it. In such cases, the government would be left with an unattractive set of fiscal policy choices: raise taxes, cut spending, and borrow money.

How do stablecoins work?

Most stablecoins work like the gold standard worked for millennia: they are structured to give users confidence that they are supported by, and on some level can be exchanged into, a particular type of collateral. While that is true for most stablecoins, another type of stablecoin has emerged that is not collateralized and uses principles of supply and demand to maintain a stable price. Such coins, called seigniorage or algorithmic stablecoins, while interesting in theory, have not yet been adopted at scale.

For the collateralized stablecoins, two main types have emerged:

- traditional asset-backed stablecoins, collateralized by physical assets such as fiat currencies (US dollar, euro, Japanese yen) or commodities such as gold or oil; and

- crypto-backed stablecoins, collateralized by other crypto.

Traditional Asset-Backed Stablecoins

The most popular traditional asset-backed stablecoins are collateralized with hard assets and run by centralized entities. Their value depends on the value of the underlying collateral, and often are designed to be pegged to a fiat currency like the US dollar (1 unit = $1.00). This section will use Tether, a centralized, asset-backed stablecoin as an example. Tether's owners also operate the crypto exchange Bitfinex.

The price of one tether (USD₮) is designed to be pegged to the US dollar, meaning each 1 USD₮ should maintain a value of $1.00. In order to maintain the peg, Tether must convince the broader market that it has sufficient collateral to support all the USD₮ that has been issued. That means that at any time, the market must believe all issued and outstanding USD₮ can be exchanged 1:1 for dollars, or, at minimum, one dollar's worth of collateral.

In the last five years, the price of USD₮ have remained relatively stable, reaching a high of about $1.015 in 2017 and a low of around $0.9625 in late 2018, but generally maintaining the 1:1 peg with the dollar. Tether has maintained its stability despite questions arising in 2019 regarding its collateral, based on two incidents:

Incident 1: Collateral Questions

Prior to February 2019, Tether's website provided the following information about its collateral:

> *Every tether is always backed 1-to-1, by traditional currency held in our reserves. Thus, 1 USD₮ is always equivalent to [$1 dollar].*

In March 2019, Tether's website was updated, and stated:

> *Every tether is always 100% backed by our reserves, which include traditional currency and cash equivalents **and, from time to time, may include other assets and receivables from loans made by Tether to third parties, which may include affiliated entities (collectively, "reserves")***

That updated information raised the possibility that Tether was not fully collateralized. Moreover, the inclusion of language about "other assets"—which literally could be anything—caused many in the crypto community to question both the quality and sufficiency of Tether's collateral, and raised doubts about whether there was sufficient collateral for all the USD₮ in circulation.

Incident 2: Missing Collateral

In April 2019, the New York attorney general's office alleged that Bitfinex (Tether's sister company) used $850 million of Tether's collateral to cover up $850 million that was somehow "missing" from Bitfinex's accounts. Bitfinex has contended that the funds were not missing but had been seized by government authorities. The matter was argued in front of an appeals court in New York in March 2020, and a ruling is expected later in 2020.

Despite those two incidents, according to the stablecoin index (stablecoinindex.com), Tether has continued to maintain its peg to the dollar and remains the stablecoin with the highest market capitalization. Whether Tether will maintain its dominance is anyone's guess. However, a new competitor has plans to compete in the stablecoin market.

Enter Facebook

 On June 18, 2019, Facebook announced that it would offer a fiat-backed stablecoin called "Libra." According to the announcement, Libra was expected to go live sometime in 2020 and would be collateralized by a basket of relatively stable currencies, likely including the US dollar, the euro, and the Japanese yen.

Facebook's announcement was significant because Libra could easily become the world's leading stablecoin if enough of the 1.7 billion active Facebook account holders decided to use Libra. Libra's future success, as well as its long-term impact, are clearly unknown. However, Facebook's announcement raised some important questions, including:

- *How will Facebook deal with user privacy?*

- *Will Facebook accounts be linked to Libra accounts?*

- *Will Libra be decentralized, and if not, is it really a crypto?*

- *Who will make decisions for Libra, and how will those decisions be made?*

- *Would a currency based on developed-world currencies necessarily mean that the rest of the world would be beholden to, and subject to manipulation by, developed-world central bankers?*

- *Should monetary policy be controlled, in whole or in part, by corporate entities (or, as was stated in a Bloomberg opinion piece, "a cabal of tech czars and venture capitalists")?*

- *What power will governments have to force Libra to exclude people, or people from certain nations, from using it? For example, could the United States force Libra to exclude North Koreans and Iranians?*

The reaction to the Libra announcement was mixed. US Congressman Darren Soto, co-chair of the Congressional Blockchain Caucus, stated:

> *"We are encouraged by the possibility of increasing access to mobile and digital payments, which will ultimately benefit our society and become a driver of*

economic growth. While it is yet unclear how this new technology will be regulated, it is crucial Congress continues to protect consumers and the financial well-being of investors, while simultaneously promoting innovation for these virtual currencies."

Others in Congress were not so enthusiastic. Sherrod Brown, a member of the Senate Banking Committee, tweeted:

"Facebook is already too big and too powerful, and it has used that power to exploit users' data without protecting their privacy . . . We cannot allow Facebook to run a risky new cryptocurrency out of a Swiss bank account without oversight."

Around the world, the reaction was also mixed:

- On September 13, 2019, France and Germany issued a joint statement on Libra, which stated:

  "We believe that no private entity can claim monetary power, which is inherent to the sovereignty of nations."

- France's finance minister Bruno Le Maire said that Libra "can't and . . . must not happen" and that "it is out of question" for the cryptocurrency to "become a sovereign currency."

- Bank of England governor Mark Carney said he was open-minded about Libra, but warned mass adoption would force it "to be subject to the highest standards of regulation."

- Australia's central bank chief Philip Lowe said, "there are a lot of regulatory issues that need to be addressed and they've got to make sure there's a solid business case, so we've got to be careful before we jump to conclusions."

The zodiac stablecoins: life imitates astrology

Other interesting facts in the Libra launch can be found in *Bitcoin Billionaires*, a book by Ben Mezrich, the same author who wrote *The Accidental Billionaires: The Founding of Facebook*, the book behind the 2010 film *The Social Network*. In *Bitcoin Billionaires*, Mezrich chronicles the first Bitcoin billionaire twins, the Winklevosses, who, along with Mark Zuckerburg, were involved in the creation of Facebook. The book also describes the falling out between Zuckerburg and the Winklevosses, citing the Winklevosses' allegation that Zuckerburg stole many of the ideas behind Facebook from them.

Interestingly, those same Winklevoss twins created Gemini, one of the first fiat-backed stablecoins. Then, a few years after the Winklevosses created Gemini, Zuckerburg's Facebook created its own stablecoin and named it after another zodiac sign. Whether the name Libra was chosen to troll the Winklevosses is anyone's guess.

Crypto-Backed Stablecoins

Crypto-backed stablecoins rely primarily on other types of crypto as collateral, instead of fiat currencies of other non-digital assets. Most crypto-backed stablecoins are also decentralized, meaning there is no need for a centralized third-party (like those who control Tether) to maintain the stablecoin's peg.

To minimize the impact of volatility, stablecoin projects use myriad mechanisms to create price stability, but almost all rely on overcollateralization as a primary means to maintain their pegs. The following simplified example demonstrates how overcollateralization works.[10]

Stablebucks: The *Short & Happy* Stablecoin

 Let's assume Chaun, the project developer, creates a crypto-collateralized stablecoin project using smart contracts named "Stablebucks," which requires 200 percent (two-to-one) overcollateralization using bitcoin. Chaun designs the Stablebucks so that each Stablebuck is pegged to the dollar (1 Stablebuck = $1).

Users can create Stablebucks by staking (depositing) bitcoin collateral into the system, and, in return, receiving Stablebucks. Because of Stablebucks' two-to-one overcollateralization, if Bibi stakes 1 BTC into the Stablebucks smart contract (assume January 2020 price of 1 BTC = $10,000), the Stablebucks smart contract will issue her 5,000 Stablebucks, worth $5,000.

To ensure that the Stablebucks always are worth at least $1, the smart contract will be designed to sell Bibi's 1 BTC collateral if the value of that collateral falls to $5,000. In such case, the smart contract will sell the BTC and hold the $5,000, thereby ensuring that the 5,000 Stablebucks issued to Bibi are always fully collateralized and backed by $5,000 worth of assets. Once the smart contract sells the 1 BTC for $5,000, it would hold $5,000 of collateral and Bibi would have 5,000 Stablebucks, but no BTC.

Why would anyone want to risk their crypto to create a Stablebuck?

---

[10] This example is adapted from *Understanding Stablecoins from an Economist's Perspective,* published by Jan Simek in the Good Audience blog on November 22, 2018.

Leverage.[11] The Stablebuck system is a lot like a pawn shop, whereby the system is in reality making a loan based on the value of collateral staked. The person staking the collateral can use the loaned cash for any purpose, and like in the pawn shop relationship, that person generally has a greater need for the loaned proceeds than he or she has for the collateral asset.

In finance, borrowing against assets is a form of leverage. Leverage is advantageous for borrowers who believe the borrowed funds will generate profits higher than the borrowing costs.

In the Stablebucks example, assume Bibi believes the price of bitcoin will increase in the future. If she takes the 5,000 Stablebucks and uses it to purchase 0.5 BTC (at 1 BTC = $10,000), she would then have a 1.5 BTC position: 1 BTC in the Stablebucks smart contract and 0.5 BTC in her wallet.

If the price of BTC increases to 1 BTC = $20,000 (a 100 percent increase in price), Bibi's profits will be greater than 100 percent, because she used leverage to increase her position. Here's how:

> at the 1 BTC = $20,000 price, Bibi could close out the smart contract, by (1) selling 0.25 BTC for $5,000, then (2) using that $5,000 (plus whatever interest has accrued) to redeem her Stablebucks.

At that point, she would have 1.25 BTC worth $25,000, minus any interest costs. Without the Stablebucks, she would have had 1 BTC worth $20,000. Bibi's use of leverage through Stablebucks allowed her to earn a 150 percent return (ignoring interest) on the 100 percent increase in the price of bitcoin. Obviously, the costs of borrowing would reduce Bibi's return.

---

[11] Leverage is a strategy of using other people's property (OPP) to increase the potential return from an investment. Leverage increases the risk of an investment because OPP must be repaid whether the investment is profitable or not. Leverage has been around for as long as people have borrowed money. Leverage has been around for millennia, but the OPP concept was introduced to the world by Naughty by Nature in 1991.

Leverage is not always beneficial, however. If the price of BTC falls, Bibi's position will lose value faster than she would have without leverage. For example, assuming Bibi, as in the example above, created 5,000 Stablebucks, but the price of BTC decreased to 1 BTC = $7,500 (a 25 percent decrease in price). In that situation, Bibi's losses would be greater than 25 percent. At the 1 BTC = $7,500 price, to close out the smart contract, Bibi would:

1) sell 0.67 BTC for $5,000, then

2) use that $5,000 (plus interest) to redeem her Stablebucks.

At that point, she will have 0.83 BTC worth $6,225 (minus interest), a 37.75 percent loss based on a 25 percent decrease in BTC price. Without the Stablebucks, she would have had 1 BTC worth $7,500.

The examples above show the risks, and opportunities, of using stablecoins for leverage.

Why would anyone want to risk their crypto using leverage?

As Meek Mill said so eloquently, "scared money don't make no money."[12] Speculation on the price of assets has existed since at least 1750 BCE in Mesopotamia, and the Code of Hammurabi included provisions for delivery of futures-type contracts.[13] Stablecoins, like futures markets in general, increase the efficiency of the underlying crypto markets.

Maker and DAI

One of the most active crypto-backed stablecoins is DAI, a token that uses overcollateralization and another token, Maker (MKR), to maintain a 1-to-1 peg to

---

[12] *Ima Boss*, Meek Mill featuring Rick Ross, Dreamchasers (2011).

[13] More formal futures markets began in the 1700s when Japan organized the first rice futures markets.

the dollar. Initially, DAI were collateralized only by ETH (the Ethereum token), but in late 2019, the Maker/DAI system was expanded to allow for other types of collateral, creating multi-collateral DAI. The details of the Maker/DAI system are, quite frankly, complicated, but an abbreviated version is included below.[14]

How DAI and MKR work: the VERY simplified version

If Bibi wants to create DAI, Bibi would need to post crypto collateral and create a collateralized debt position (CDP), which is a smart contract in the Maker/DAI system. The amount of DAI created is based on the amount of collateral put into the CDP, and must be greater than the amount of DAI to be created. For example, if the system set the collateral ratio at 150 percent, then Bibi would have to post crypto collateral worth $150 to mint (create) 100 DAI (worth $100).

To ensure that the Maker/DAI system is robust enough to deal with the volatility of crypto, the Maker/DAI developers added additional mechanisms designed to maintain the peg between DAI and the dollar. Among those mechanisms are:

1) a stability fee, paid when the CDP is closed out (akin to the borrowing costs in the Stablebucks example above);

2) the ability to liquidate CDPs as necessary; and

3) the Maker token (MKR).[15]

---

[14] There are a number of other stability mechanisms involved in the Maker/DAI system. In order to provide an overview and keep this short, many of those mechanisms are omitted. However, for readers who want a more thorough explanation of the Maker/DAI system, please read the MakerDAO whitepaper, available at https://makerdao.com/da/whitepaper/.

[15] Other stabilization mechanisms include a liquidation penalty for CDPs that are forcibly liquidated, and a DAI Savings Rate (DSR) paid on deposits in specific DAI savings contracts.

In the Maker/DAI system, the CDPs collect a fee (stability fee), which is calculated against the total amount of DAI minted and drawn against collateral held in a CDP. In the above example, if Bibi, using her $150 in crypto collateral, minted and extracted 100 DAI, the system would charge Bibi a stability fee based on the 100 DAI extracted.

The stability fee is designed to address the risk of imbalances in supply and demand for DAI to support the peg. For example, if DAI is consistently above one dollar, it signals that demand for DAI is outweighing supply. At such time, the stability fee (borrowing cost) could be lowered to incentivize people to create CDPs and mint DAI, thereby increasing supply to meet demand.

Alternatively, if DAI is consistently below one dollar, it signals supply for DAI is outweighing demand. At such time, the stability fee (borrowing cost) could be raised, which increases the costs associated with minting and/or holding DAI, creating an incentive for people to close out their CDPs and reduce supply. The stability fee has seen significant fluctuation since the Maker/DAI system was created. It was initially set at 0.5 percent and has reached a high of 20.5 percent.[16]

The most easily explained way the Maker/DAI system maintains the peg is by liquidating CDPs if the value of the collateral falls below a certain threshold, thereby reducing the risk that the crypto collateral could be worth less than the DAI created based on that collateral. Each CDP is created based on the then-current crypto prices, and the Maker/DAI system collectively is based on the weighted average of all the crypto held in CDPs. Based on the example above, if the value of the $150 of crypto collateral held in the CDP approached $100, the system could sell the CDP before the price fell below $100 to ensure that the collateral in the system

---

[16] https://mkr.tools/governance/stabilityfee.

would always be worth more than the $100 of DAI created by that CDP.

While the stability fee and the liquidation of CDPs work to keep DAI pegged to the dollar in most circumstances, neither would work in the event of a sudden large drop in crypto prices. In such cases, it might be impossible to liquidate CDPs before the value in those CDPs fell below the amount of DAI created, which would make it difficult or impossible to maintain the peg. To address that risk, Maker/DAI system uses MKR tokens.

MKR tokens are the governance mechanism for the Maker/DAI system, and funds raised by issuing MKR tokens provide additional collateral for the Maker/DAI system to maintain the peg. MKR token holders, in addition to providing collateral to the system, are empowered to vote on issues that affect the growth and stability of the Maker/DAI system. That system incentivizes them to carefully monitor the system, and, in return, earn fees for their work.

PART III

Blockchains and the Law

Regulating the Blockchain Space

No government can claim exclusive jurisdiction over blockchain technology and crypto. However, once people started using blockchains as money (crypto), governments (i) began to apply "rules"[1] for their use, and (ii) discovered the difficulties in regulating a technology that exists outside of physical boundaries and identities.

Broadly speaking, governments have taken three approaches in regulating crypto:

Encouraging: Governments taking this approach have enacted rules supporting and encouraging crypto, making it easier for their citizens and businesses to use crypto and operate crypto businesses. A few of the more crypto-friendly countries include Malta, Japan, Bermuda, Hong Kong, Switzerland, and Singapore.

---

[1] "Rules" will be used throughout this section generally to represent laws, regulations, and other guidance, both in the US and abroad.

Malta, a tiny southern European country of about 450,000 citizens, has been an international leader in actively encouraging crypto businesses. In February 2018, the Maltese government enacted the Malta Digital Innovation Authority (MDIA), which established a comprehensive regulatory framework for crypto businesses. Later in 2018, Binance, one of the world's largest crypto exchanges by volume, relocated its headquarters from Hong Kong to Malta.

Permissive: Governments taking this approach have allowed blockchain technologies to operate, but have generally:

- instituted difficult- or expensive-to-follow rules; and/or
- failed to provide regulatory clarity, leaving citizens and businesses uncertain about whether, and under what circumstances, existing rules apply to crypto.

The US falls into this category. Although US crypto rules are generally permissive, uncertainty surrounding US regulation has been a factor in many crypto businesses relocating to non-US domiciles.

Strict: These governments have generally been hostile to crypto, banning the use or ownership of crypto, initial coin offerings, and crypto exchanges. Some of the more crypto-unfriendly countries include Algeria, Bolivia, Morocco, Nepal, Pakistan, and Vietnam.

Crypto in China

China's approach to crypto is in parts permissive, and in others parts strict. Under current law, China bans all ICOs, prohibits financial institutions from transacting in crypto, disallows patents for any

crypto-related payment technology, and, until recently, had threatened to ban crypto mining.

In April 2019, the Chinese government included bitcoin mining as an industry that it planned to phase out over time. However, in October 2019, President Xi Jinping gave a speech that called for increased efforts in blockchain development. Following that speech, the government removed crypto mining from the industries it wanted to phase out.

Around the world, crypto mining generated over $5.4 billion in revenue in 2019, and estimates suggest that between 65-81 percent of that mining activity happens in China, based on China's cheap electricity, labor, and resources. The chart below, courtesy of the *Wall Street Journal*, shows the market share of the most popular bitcoin mining pools.

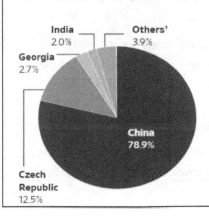

In December 2019, Mu Changchun, head of the People's Bank of China (PBoC), announced that China would soon offer a digital form of the Chinese yuan, its official currency, and that pilot programs were underway with an expected rollout in 2020. In July 2019,

> Wang Xin, the director of the PBoC Research Bureau, admitted that Facebook's announcement of the Libra stablecoin was an important factor in China's interest in bringing the digital yuan to the market. Many have speculated that a digital yuan could help China challenge the global supremacy of the US dollar.

Despite the disparate regulatory approaches to crypto, world governments have long-cooperated in establishing rules to protect the integrity of the international financial system. The current effort began in earnest in 1989, when the Financial Action Task Force (FATF) was organized to set standards and promote effective implementation of legal, regulatory, and operational rules to prevent money laundering (anti-money laundering or AML) and combat other forms of financial crimes. The FATF mandate was expanded after the September 11, 2001, attacks in the US to include methods to combat terrorist financing (CTF).

What is The Financial Action Task Force?

 FATF sets standards and promotes effective implementation of legal, regulatory, and operational measures for combating money laundering, terrorist financing, and other related threats to the integrity of the international financial system. According to the FATF website:

- FATF is a policy-making body which works to generate the necessary political will to bring about national legislative and regulatory reforms.

- FATF monitors the progress of its members in implementing necessary legal, regulatory, and operational measures for combating money laundering, terrorist financing, and other related threats to the integrity of the international financial system.

- In collaboration with other international stakeholders, FATF works to identify national-level vulnerabilities with the aim of protecting the international financial system from misuse.

FATF has thirty-nine member countries, including the US, China, and the European Commission (which represents the EU). In addition, the following intergovernmental groups, whose missions are generally to frustrate money laundering, are associate members of FATF:

- Asia/Pacific Group on Money Laundering
- Caribbean Financial Action Task Force
- Council of Europe Committee of Experts on the Evaluation of Anti-Money Laundering Measures and the Financing of Terrorism
- Eurasian Group
- Eastern and Southern Africa Anti-Money Laundering Group
- Financial Action Task Force of Latin America
- Inter-Governmental Action Group against Money Laundering in West Africa
- Middle East and North Africa Financial Action Task Force
- Task Force on Money Laundering in Central Africa

International organizations with an anti-money laundering focus also work with FATF and serve as observers, including the World Bank, the United Nations, Interpol, the Organization of Economic

> Co-operation and Development (OECD), and the International Monetary Fund, among others.

In 2014, FATF made a preliminary assessment of the money laundering and terror financing risks of crypto (crypto are referred to as "virtual currencies" by FATF). Then in 2015, FATF provided guidance aimed at helping countries develop rules to manage crypto-related AML/CTF risks. The 2015 guidance called upon countries to assess the types of AML/CTF risks crypto represented, and to implement rules to prevent the use of crypto for money laundering and terrorist financing.

FATF's guidance was updated in October 2018 to broaden its scope. That update included guidance that clarified that crypto business and services, called "virtual asset service providers" (VASPs) by FATF, should be subject to AML/CTF rules. FATF specifically listed crypto exchanges, wallet providers, and providers of financial services for ICOs as examples of VASPs. The 2018 guidance also set out compliance standards for issuers, guidelines for ICOs, and directions for banks, securities dealers, and other financial institutions involved with crypto.

In June 2019, FATF finalized its AML/CTF guidelines, called "FATF Recommendations," that laid out explicit rules for governments to implement. The FATF Recommendations proposed that:

- companies or individuals that are VASPs be licensed or registered in the jurisdictions they were created;

- countries take legal or regulatory measures to prevent criminals from owning or controlling VASPs;

- VASPs not be self-regulated;

- VASPs be subject to AML/CTF regulation, supervision, and monitoring;

- VASPs provide identity information to relevant authorities and keep track of the counterparties to crypto transfers over $1,000 (or 1,000EUR) and, when requested:

  o share that information with appropriate authorities, and

  o if a transaction is suspect, give regulators the power to take appropriate action, including prohibiting the transfer or freezing the assets;

  and

- regulators be given the power to inspect, compel document production, and sanction VASPs, and those sanctions should include administrative, civil, and/or criminal penalties.

Do governments have to follow FATF Recommendations?

FATF Recommendations are not law. They do, however, act as a kind of "soft law," i.e., rules that perform like laws because the consequences of non-compliance can be costly. Soft laws are akin to an admonition not to touch a hot stove.

Although FATF Recommendations do not have the legal standing or enforceability of treaties or customary international law, member governments are nevertheless incentivized to comply with them because the consequences for non-compliance are substantial. Governments that fail to comply with FATF Recommendations can be added to a list of non-cooperating countries, warranting what FATF calls "special attention."

FATF "special attention" includes close examination of a non-cooperating country's international business transactions, potential downgrades of a non-cooperating country's debt, and restrictions on a non-cooperating country's ability to get aid from the

International Monetary Fund or the World Bank, both FATF observer members. In some circumstances, non-cooperating countries can be prohibited from participating in global financial arrangements like SWIFT and other forms of global clearing and settlement. If non-compliance were severe enough, that "special attention" could also include economic sanctions.

The FATF Recommendations represent a multilateral approach to regulation, and, as with most such approaches, member countries have a great deal of flexibility in actually implementing them.

> *"The more important the financial center, the less likely it is to hand over control of its regulatory regime to an international organization like FATF."*

—Jake Chervinsky, General Counsel, *Compound Finance*

It should come as no surprise that the amount of a country's flexibility correlates strongly with its economic power and importance. This is especially true of the US, because FinCEN, the US agency most responsible for implementing FATF Recommendations, has generally adopted only the FATF Recommendations it agreed with and ignored the others.

US Law and Regulation

This section and the following chapters explore the US regulation of financial transactions involving crypto, including:

Money Law: state and federal rules for financial institutions, money transmitters and financial service businesses;

Financial Products Law: rules relating to crypto from the Securities and Exchange Commission (SEC) and the Commodity Futures Trading Commission (CFTC); and

Tax Law: rules promulgated by the IRS relating to the taxation of crypto.

Despite the generally permissive approach to crypto regulation in the US, regulatory uncertainty has put the US at a competitive disadvantage with other nations. That uncertainty exists because, unlike most other countries, the US has multiple regulators that have asserted jurisdiction over crypto. As a result, absent a coordinated federal framework for regulation, various federal agencies and all 53 state and territorial governments (the 50 states, plus DC, Puerto Rico, and Guam) have to power to, and in some instance have, regulated certain aspects of crypto.

Federal regulation

In the US, the following agencies have asserted jurisdiction over crypto:

- Commodity Futures Trading Commission (CFTC)
- Federal Deposit Insurance Commission (FDIC)
- Federal Reserve Board (the Fed)
- Office of the Comptroller of the Currency (OCC)
- US Securities and Exchange Commission (SEC)
- US Treasury Department (Treasury), including the following units:
  o Office of Foreign Assets Control (OFAC)
  o Financial Crimes Enforcement Network (FinCEN)
  o Internal Revenue Service (IRS)
  o Office of Financial Research (OFR)

Among those federal regulators, there is little consistency in how crypto is characterized. For instance,

- the SEC treats some crypto as securities;

- the CFTC treats some crypto as commodities; and

- separate Treasury units have separate treatments, for example:

  o   FinCEN generally treats crypto as money;

  o   the IRS treats crypto as property; and

  o   OFAC treats crypto as virtual currencies.

There is no easy way to explain comprehensively the regulatory treatment of crypto in a book with a title that includes the words "Short & Happy." The remainder of the book does, however, provide examples and analysis of how both federal and state regulators have dealt with crypto, and provides the reader with a roadmap for further investigation. This book concludes with an overview of legislative proposals aimed at providing more clarity to crypto regulation.

Money Law

Any discussion of the regulations regarding financial transactions begins with the Bank Secrecy Act (BSA). The BSA, passed in 1970 and amended by the Patriot Act in 2001, is the most comprehensive federal AML/CTF statute. The BSA mandates that financial services businesses collect and retain information about their customers, share that information with appropriate authorities, and create specific procedures for reporting "suspicious" activities or face significant penalties.

FinCEN is the Treasury bureau whose mission is to safeguard the financial system from illicit use, combat money laundering, and promote national security through financial intelligence. FinCEN is also the primary regulator enforcing the BSA.

According to the FinCEN website:

> *the Bank Secrecy Act authorizes the Secretary of the Treasury to issue regulations requiring banks and other financial institutions to take a number of precautions against financial crime, including the establishment of AML programs and the filing of reports that have been determined to have a high degree of usefulness in criminal, tax, and regulatory investigations and proceedings, and certain intelligence and counter-terrorism matters. The Secretary of the Treasury has delegated to the Director of FinCEN the authority to implement, administer, and enforce compliance with the BSA and associated regulations.*

The BSA represents a policy choice by the US government to effectively deputize financial service businesses to surveil their customers' financial activities in an effort to prevent crime. As with many government policies, the BSA is a tradeoff between security and privacy. Without delving into the respective merits of the security/privacy debate (again), the broad policy issues are as follows:

Security Position

In an effort to stop crime, protect their citizens, and thwart terrorism, governments assert the need to track the movement of crypto to prevent criminals from being able to spend illegally obtained funds and prevent individuals from financing terrorism.

Privacy Position

Information about financial accounts is uniquely private, and allowing a government access to an individual's financial accounts without demonstrating a clear need for that information (generally by showing probable cause or reasonable suspicion in the US) violates an individual's right to privacy and limits an individual's freedom.

As noted in Part II, an oft-cited fact in this debate is the increased use of crypto in criminal activity. For example, in 2019 CipherTrace reported that 76 percent of "dark market" (see box below) and ransomware transactions used bitcoin for payment.

The use of crypto in criminal activity appears to be escalating. According to *Forbes* magazine and CipherTrace, in the first six months of 2019, crypto "thefts, scams, and fraud worldwide" netted criminals over $4.25 billion (to have access to that money, criminals must launder[2] the money), compared to $1.7 billion over the entire 2018 year.

Dark Markets

Dark markets (or darknets) are websites where illegal products and services are traded. In general, dark market transactions are conducted over the Tor network and are anonymized. The currency for many dark market transactions is often crypto, either bitcoin or privacy coins. In many dark markets, payments are held in escrow by the site operator to discourage scammers. Silk Road was the most popular dark market until it was shut down in 2013 by the FBI. Soon thereafter, AlphaBay emerged as the most popular darknet until it was shut down in 2017 as part of a joint US, Canadian, and Thai effort.

Many in the crypto community counter that the money laundered in crypto pales in comparison to the amounts laundered through traditional financial institutions, citing the International Monetary Fund's annual money laundering estimate of $600 billion to $1.5 trillion. Needless to say, the debate continues.

FinCEN's Rules

On May 9, 2019, FinCEN issued guidance regarding crypto (described in its guidance as "convertible virtual currencies" (CVCs)). Before

---

2 Money laundering is the process of attempting to disguise the proceeds of illegal activity in an attempt to make those proceeds appear to have originated from legitimate sources. For a fictionalized, but nonetheless accurate, portrayal of money laundering in practice, watch the Netflix series *Ozarks*.

discussing the contours of FinCEN's guidance, it is important to understand the role of guidance in US regulation.

Regulatory Guidance

Guidance is material published by a regulatory agency that helps clarify existing rules, and generally represents the agency's position on how the existing laws and regulations *should* apply. According to FinCEN, its guidance should "clarify issues or respond to questions of general applicability that arise under FinCEN regulations."

Guidance cannot be relied on in a court of law, but can be used to persuade a court regarding an agency's position. Agencies often issue guidance when they are unwilling or unable to issue regulations, or when they want to broadcast a policy position to the public. Guidance is easier to issue than regulations because if an agency wants to issue regulations, in most cases the agency must draft proposed regulations, distribute the proposals to the public, and provide the public with the opportunity to comment on them (called "Notice and Comment"). Under federal law, non-binding guidance is exempted from Notice and Comment under the Administrative Procedures Act.

Although guidance does not have the force of law, it is another example of "soft law" that carries persuasive weight and often serves as unofficial regulation. Critics of agency guidance often claim that agencies use guidance to expand the scope of their authority, or to make public policy in the absence of congressional direction. Although regulatory agencies are part of the executive branch, some members of the post-Obama administration complained that guidance sometimes serves as "a back door for regulators" to frustrate executive branch decisions.

FinCEN's guidance explained circumstances in which FinCEN would subject crypto businesses to the same registration, recordkeeping, reporting, AML and know your customer (KYC) requirements as other traditional money services businesses (for example, Western Union). While the definitions of what types of crypto activity would be subject to the AML/KYC requirements are detailed, those definitions generally state that if a business or service accepts something valuable (such as crypto) and transmits it to another person, entity or location, then that business or service is a money transmitter, and therefore must follow the BSA's AML/KYC requirements.

In May 2019, FinCEN issued its most game-changing guidance regarding crypto, requiring crypto businesses, including exchanges and service providers, to follow the Funds Travel Rule, a longstanding part of FinCEN's non-crypto anti-money laundering efforts.[3] Based on FATF Recommendation 16, the Funds Travel Rule requires that either before or at the time of a transaction, financial intermediaries must obtain, hold, and transmit information about the originators and beneficiaries of funds transfers over $3,000 (or the equivalent in crypto). That information must include:

ORIGINATOR	BENEFICIARY
• name • account number, if used • address • identity of originator's financial institution • amount sent • execution date, and • identity of beneficiary's financial institution	• name • account number, if used • address • any other specific identifying information

---

[3]   The Funds Travel Rule was arguably expanded to apply to crypto in 2013 with an amendment to include electronic funds transfers, but absent specific guidance regarding its application to crypto, it had been routinely ignored.

The Funds Travel Rule also gives financial intermediaries the ability to monitor transactions and requires them to report suspicious transactions to the government. Together, the BSA and the Funds Travel empower the government and financial intermediaries to take what they deem is appropriate action regarding suspicious activities, including freezing accounts and prohibiting transactions with designated persons or entities.

While the coverage of the Funds Travel Rule is certainly broad, there are exceptions. Generally, if crypto is sent outside of the financial intermediary system, the Funds Travel Rule will not apply. That exception applies to:

- transactions where customers control the funds ("unhosted" wallets or cold wallets) and conduct transactions on their own behalf;

- peer-to-peer transactions between individuals or non-financial intermediaries; and

- peer-to-peer transactions on crypto trading platforms that enable buyers and sellers to find each other, so long as the trading platform only provides a forum for posting bids and offers, and the parties themselves settle any matched transactions through an outside venue (either through individual wallets or other wallets not hosted by the trading platform).

Many in the crypto community criticized FinCEN's decision to apply the Funds Travel Rule to crypto, for both policy and practical reasons:

Policy

The Funds Travel Rule is contrary to the underlying principles of decentralization and privacy that blockchain technologies are built upon. In addition, circumventing the Funds Travel Rule through the use of individual (non-VASP) accounts or peer-to-peer services will be fairly straightforward, and instead of reducing money laundering, it will only increase the compliance costs of legitimate actors in the crypto industry.

Practical

Because crypto transactions are pseudonymous, blockchain transactions do not intrinsically contain, collect or capture the data needed to comply with the Funds Travel Rule. In fact, modifying blockchain protocols to allow for the capture that data would undermine the privacy, confidentiality and coding efficiency of many crypto protocols. Moreover, miners and developers have no incentive to make modifications that decrease the privacy associated with public blockchains.

In November 2019, a coordinated worldwide effort to comply with the Funds Travel Rule and FATF Recommendation 16 was organized by a number of crypto-focused industry associations, called the "OpenVASP initiative." According to its press release, the project "will enable VASPs to transmit blockchain transaction information privately, immediately and securely, in compliance with [FATF Recommendation 16 and the Funds Travel Rule]." The OpenVASP initiative white paper states that its protocol will be "based on key design principles of decentralization, privacy, broad applicability, while remaining agnostic to the virtual asset being transferred," and would allow VASPs from across multiple jurisdictions to transact between themselves without necessarily knowing each other and without the need to register with a central authority or database.

Concerns raised about the initiative include:

- the protocol would immediately become a honeypot for hackers, as it would contain a global list of detailed financial information; and

- if it were shut down (for example because of a distributed denial of service attack), money transmissions could be frozen until the system was back online.

Despite concerns about implementing the Funds Travel Rule, in November 2019 FinCEN Director Kenneth Blanco warned crypto businesses that if they claim their technology cannot comply, they will not be able to do business in the US. Blanco also stated that the US government would "strictly enforce" the Funds Travel Rule, adding:

> "[The Funds Travel Rule] applies to [crypto] and we expect that you will comply period. That's what our expectation is. You will comply. I don't know what the shock is. This is nothing new."

Many crypto exchanges began implementing AML/KYC policies in response to FinCEN's guidance. As discussed in the ShapeShift box below, such implementation has not been without controversy.

The Case of ShapeShift

 ShapeShift is a crypto exchange designed to allow users to "quickly swap between assets in a seamless, safe, and secure environment." ShapeShift was founded in 2014 by Erik Voorhees, and until 2018, allowed users to exchange crypto on a peer-to-peer basis without providing any account information. ShapeShift touted itself as providing its users with the maximum level of consumer protection and efficiency, and

banned the use of fiat currency on its platform as a way to avoid US AML/KYC regulations.

However, shortly after the *Wall Street Journal* reported that $9 million in fraudulently-obtained funds had been laundered through its platform, ShapeShift introduced mandatory AML/KYC policies for all users. In discussing that shift in policy, Voorhees stated:

> *"I personally and us as a company respect the right of individuals to have financial privacy. Forcing KYC on people violates that right. So I don't support that. The fact that we are doing it isn't because we support that. It's because we are essentially being forced to do that."*

> —*WhatBitcoinDid* podcast March 20, 2019

Know Your Customer

In addition to AML policies, FinCEN guidance and the BSA also require financial institutions to implement KYC policies to help financial institutions avoid illicit transactions by improving their ability to monitor and observe their clients' identities and business relationships. The KYC regulations:

1) set forth rules for a financial institution's customer due diligence (CDD) program;

2) require financial institutions to verify the legal identity and/or beneficial ownership (see box below) of all customers, whether individuals or entities, when new accounts are opened; and

3) mandate that a financial institution's CDD programs include procedures for:

    (i) monitoring and reporting suspicious activities, and

(ii) maintaining and updating customer information.

Who is a "Beneficial Owner"

The FinCEN definition of a beneficial owner casts a wide net. According to FinCEN, a beneficial owner is:

1. Each individual, if any, who, directly or indirectly, through any contract, arrangement, understanding, relationship or otherwise, owns 25 percent or more of the equity interests of a legal entity customer.

2. A single individual with significant responsibility to control, manage, or direct a legal entity customer, including:

    (i) an executive officer or senior manager (e.g., a Chief Executive Officer, Chief Financial Officer, Chief Operating Officer, Managing Member, General Partner, President, Vice President, or Treasurer); or

    (ii) any other individual who regularly performs similar functions.

3. If a trust owns directly or indirectly, through any contract, arrangement, understanding, relationship or otherwise, 25 percent or more of the equity interests of a legal entity customer, the beneficial owner shall mean the trustee.

In addition to collecting the beneficial ownership information, KYC regulations require financial institutions to screen the names of beneficial owners through OFAC's lists of Specially Designated Nationals and Blocked Persons (SDN), which identifies:

- individuals and companies owned or controlled by, or acting for or on behalf of, targeted countries; and

- individuals, groups, and entities, such as terrorists and narcotics traffickers designated under programs that are not country-specific.

The assets of SDNs are blocked and US persons are generally prohibited from dealing with them.

Unintended Consequences of KYC

Notwithstanding privacy issues, some have argued that KYC requirements prevent certain groups, particularly the poor and those without existing banking relationships (the unbanked), from participating in the financial system. For example, between 2011 and 2013, many banks in the UK and the US took the pre-emptive step of closing all Somalia-based money service business accounts based on the risk that those accounts could be linked to terror organizations like al-Shabaab, which operated out of Somalia.

The closing of accounts meant that individuals in the Somali diaspora living abroad could no longer send remittances back to Somalia through UK or US banks. At the time, remittances from the US alone equaled roughly $200 million per year, and accounted for roughly 40 percent of Somalia's gross domestic product.

The banks closed those accounts regardless of any actual risk or evidence of illicit activities, in order to avoid potential fines from FinCEN or the UK's Financial Conduct Authority (FCA). The banks' actions had the effect of not only crippling an already weak economy, but also empowering terror organizations.

In an April 11, 2015, New York Times editorial, US Congressman Keith Ellison argued that blocking the remittances to places like Somalia actually encouraged terror organizations. Congressman Ellison, as well as other international organizations, have argued that remittances provide financial support for families and serve as a vehicle for commercial trade, thereby limiting the appeal of terror organizations. Moreover, by closing access to money service businesses, international organizations cannot access funds to support their humanitarian missions, further encouraging terror organizations.

For many banks, however, the risk of FinCEN or FCA fines outweighed the benefits of engaging in transactions with Somali entities. On average, banks charged fees of approximately five percent per remittance, and processed between $1-$2 million per year of Somali remittances, generating roughly $50,000-$100,000 of fee revenue for the average bank. However, the potential fines from FinCEN or FCA for being linked to a terror group such as al-Shabaab could have reached into the tens or hundreds of millions.

Funds Travel Rule, Privacy Coins and Coinjoins

As noted in Part II, privacy coins and coinjoins frustrate a government's ability to track crypto transactions, by making parties to transactions appear anonymous. FinCEN's guidance states that originators or beneficiaries who use a pseudonym or account that cannot be decoded by the receiving financial institution are not in compliance with the Funds Travel Rule. Moreover, when a financial intermediary knowingly accepts anonymity-enhanced crypto (such as privacy coins or crypto that has been anonymized), financial intermediaries must not only track the crypto through different transactions, but also implement procedures to obtain the identity of the originator or beneficiary.

The Funds Travel Rule has led several regulated exchanges to begin delisting privacy coins out of fear they may violate AML regulations. For example, Coinbase in the UK delisted Zcash in August 2019, and Korea's OKEx and Upbit exchanges announced they would delist at least five privacy coins, including Zcash and DASH, in September

2019. The Coinbase delisting appears to have been driven, in part, by its new banking partner, ClearBank, demanding that the exchange delist Zcash.[4]

The OKEx and Upbit delisting announcements were driven by FATF and Funds Travel Rule concerns, and OKEx cited the Funds Travel Rule in announcing its decision. Upbit followed through on its announcement to delist the Zcash in September 2019. However, in October 2020, OKEx announced the delisting was under review, and a final decision on Zcash and DASH would be announced after that review. As of May 2020, OKEx had yet to remove Zcash trading from its platform.

Prior to 2019, it was unclear whether FinCEN would consider coinjoins and other mixers (called anonymizing services by FinCEN) as money transmitters, thus subject to AML regulations. However in 2019, FinCEN promulgated guidance clarifying when anonymizing services would be subject to FinCEN regulation. According to FinCEN, there were two types of anonymizing services:

1) <u>Services Providers</u>: either persons that accept [crypto] and retransmit them in a manner designed to prevent others from tracing the transmission back to its source, and

2) <u>Software Providers</u>: suppliers of software a transmittor would use for the same purpose.

In its 2019 guidance, FinCEN stated that anonymizing Service Providers would be considered money transmitters because such businesses are "engaged in the business of offering secure money transmission." However, anonymizing Software Providers would not be considered money transmitters, because "suppliers of tools

---

[4] Without a banking relationship, it is difficult for an exchange to operate. Coinbase UK needed a new bank because Barclays had severed its relationship with Coinbase UK, and multiple sources claimed Barclays' decision was based on the bank becoming increasingly uncomfortable with crypto.

(communications, hardware, or software) that may be utilized in money transmission, like anonymizing software, *are engaged in trade and not money transmission.*" [Emphasis supplied]

That distinction was important because prior to the guidance, it was unclear whether FinCEN was going to attempt to subject software platforms and developers of anonymizing software to AML/KYC regulations. Doing so would have defeated the purpose of anonymizing services and effectively destroyed those businesses.

While those services appear legal in the US, that is not universally the case. In December 2019, a Binance customer tweeted that the Binance Singapore exchange prevented him from withdrawing his crypto because he used a mixer. The mixer in question was the Wasabi mixing wallet, a decentralized coinjoin that does not offer third-party services that take custody of user funds, thus an anonymizing Software Provider not subject to AML regulations according to FinCEN.

The Binance action troubled many in the crypto industry, because the exchange had already followed KYC rules with the customer, meaning it appeared to be solely the use of the mixer that caused Binance to freeze the customer's account. After the customer's tweet, crypto Twitter (#CryptoTwitter, #crypto, #bitcoin) was abuzz with speculation about the reason for Binance's action. Binance CEO Changpeng Zhao (CZ) alluded that AML/CFT/KYC regulations were a reason the customer's coins were frozen. The customer was ultimately allowed to withdraw his funds, but only after promising not to deposit to a mixing wallet again.

It is likely the Binance action was the first live skirmish in a coming government battle against coinjoins and mixers, however that battle has been brewing for years. In January 2017, officials from

Europol, Interpol, and the Basel Institute on Governance[5] met to discuss crypto generally, and mixers in particular. Following the conference, the Basel Institute issued the following warning:

> *All countries are advised to take action against digital currency mixers/tumblers. Such services are designed exclusively to anonymize transactions and to make it impossible for law enforcement agencies to detect and trace suspicious transactions. The existence of such companies should not continue to be tolerated.*

---

[5]   An independent not-for-profit competence centre working around the world to strengthen governance and counter corruption and other financial crimes. See baselgovernance.org

State Laws and the UCC

In the US, commercial transaction laws are generally governed by the states. Each state has enacted laws and regulations that determine commercial transaction rules within its borders. To provide a measure of interstate consistency, all 50 states have adopted some form of the Uniform Commercial Code (described in the box below), drafted by the Uniform Law Commission.

The Uniform Commercial Code (UCC)

The UCC is a set of model laws that provides rules governing commercial or business transactions (other than real estate). The UCC was first published in 1952 by the Uniform Law Commission and has been revised numerous times over the years. Although all 50 states have adopted the UCC, jurisdictional variations exist, often related to state-specific concerns.

The UCC covers a number of transactions, including sales, leases, negotiable instruments, bank deposits and collections, funds transfers, letters of credit, bulk sales, documents of title, investment securities, and secured transactions. The main goals of the UCC are:

- to provide simple, clear rules for commercial transactions;

- to permit the continued expansion of commercial practices through custom, usage, and agreement of the parties; and

- to make the laws of commercial transactions uniform among the various states.

In 2017, the Uniform Law Commission drafted a framework for regulating crypto-related commercial business activity, called the

Uniform Regulation of Virtual Currency Businesses Act (URVCBA). In 2018, the Uniform Law Commission added a Supplemental Act to the URVCBA (collectively, the URVCBA and the Supplemental Act are referred to as the "Model Acts") that "provided commercial law rules using the time-tested duties and rights of customers of securities intermediaries under the UCC." In a statement, the Uniform Law Commission said:

> *"To meet the growing need for law on this topic, the [Uniform Law Commission and the American Law Institute] have created a study committee to determine how the [UCC] might be amended on a uniform basis to deal with emerging technologies. States are urged to refrain from enacting legislation pending the result of the committee's work.*
>
> *The study committee's process will take into account diverse views and perspectives and practical applications, and it will draw from a wide range of skills and expertise. The process is especially relevant where some technologies are at early stages or otherwise have not fully matured and creative approaches need to be devised in anticipation of, and not to stifle, future transactions and developments. The committee welcomes participants from states that wish to be involved in its work and from individuals and groups with a stake in the development of appropriate laws to govern digital-asset transactions."*

The most important UCC-related issue with respect to crypto was how crypto would be treated if held by intermediaries like brokers, financial institutions, or exchanges. Without clear UCC rules, it would be difficult for customers and intermediaries to determine true legal ownership of crypto held through intermediaries.

One potential solution was to treat crypto as "money" under the UCC, which in most circumstances deems the party that holds the money as its true legal owner. However, while bitcoin and many other crypto are often used as a form of money, UCC treatment as "money" has traditionally applied only to fiat currencies.

The Uniform Law Commission's answer was that crypto held by intermediaries would be treated like traditional securities, meaning the intermediaries would be regarded as the true legal owners.[6] Under the Model Acts, crypto "held indirectly through a bank, broker or other intermediary" was defined as "investment property" and would receive the same benefits and protections provided for indirectly-held securities under the UCC.

The Uniform Law Commission's decision to treat crypto like indirectly-held securities was not well-received by the crypto community. In fact, the debate about the Model Acts spilled onto the pages of *Forbes* magazine in a March 2019 series of articles. Soon after the articles were published, the Uniform Law Commission effectively withdrew the Model Acts, publicly announcing that states considering adopting the Model Acts should refrain from doing so, pending further study.[7]

What was the issue with the Model Acts?

The main conflict over the Model Acts was to whom commercial laws should provide the highest protection, called "super negotiability." Under the UCC, super negotiability generally means that *the holder is the true legal owner and that owner can sell* assets *held* "free and clear," without any encumbrances (in lay terms, with no strings

---

[6]   The Model Acts could have treated crypto as "general intangibles," a catch-all category for various types of personal property. General intangible treatment would have made it more difficult for intermediaries to use their customers' crypto to earn profits, as described throughout this section.

[7]   At the time of that announcement, five states had bills moving through their legislatures seeking to enact parts, or all, of the Model Acts. However, one state, Wyoming, enacted laws directly in contrast to the Model Acts.

attached), unless the purchasers knew about the encumbrances and acted to defraud the party with the encumbrance. The Model Acts' approach was to give that protection to intermediaries. Many in the crypto community believed that protection belonged to the customers.

Why is super negotiability so important?

Super negotiability allows intermediaries who have custody of a customer's property to borrow and lend that property—and earn profits from doing so—potentially without the customer's knowledge or consent. In addition, by giving intermediaries legal ownership, super negotiability means that customers are left only with a legal claim against the intermediary if the intermediary fails to return the customers' property.

How crypto super negotiability would work in practice is unclear, but the stock market provides a good starting point to make such a comparison. In the US, almost all publicly traded stock held through brokerage accounts (such as Schwab, eTrade or Robinhood) are held in "street name," meaning a customer does not actually own the stock in her or his brokerage account. Instead, customers are "beneficial" owners of "their" stock, and some other entity is the true, legal owner of the stock.[8]

The street name system was implemented because it eliminated the constant need to transfer physical stock between brokers and customers. For investors, the street name system allows for faster transactions while giving investors all the rights and benefits of being a stockholder without the burden of keeping a physical stock certificate safe from loss or theft.[9]

---

[8]   A company called Cede & Co., which is a nominee of another company called the Depository Trust Company, is often the true, legal owner of customer's stocks, and all beneficial rights such as voting rights and dividends flow first to the nominee holder Cede, and then are passed onward, and ultimately to the beneficial owners.

[9]   The street name system also provides protection against a broker's insolvency, in two ways:

Publicly traded stocks held in street name are often borrowed or lent by brokerages or other financial intermediaries, and in 2018, generated revenues of nearly $10 billion. Retail investors typically receive none of those revenues. However those revenues are a contributing factor in the significant reduction in trading fees over the last two decades.

Many within the crypto community argued that commercial law for crypto should not confer the regulatory advantage of super negotiability on intermediaries, particularly when blockchain technologies are based on disintermediation, i.e., the ability to reduce or eliminate the need for intermediaries. Moreover, many pointed out that conferring that regulatory advantage on intermediaries would create the same inefficiencies in the crypto market that occur in the stock market, using the *Dole* case (see box below) as a prime example.

134 Shareholders for every 100 Shares

The problems with the street name system were on full display in the 2017 class action lawsuit *In re Dole Food Company* (*Dole*). In *Dole*, the plaintiffs alleged that shares of the company were undervalued by management at the time of an acquisition. The lawsuit was ultimately settled, and Dole shareholders were entitled to receive $2.74 per share. And that's where things got interesting.

1. When a firm faces liquidation, regulators, including the SEC and FINRA, work to ensure that customers' securities are transferred to another firm. Keeping investments in street names may facilitate that process because beneficial ownership information is centralized.
2. As part of the street name system, the Securities Investor Protection Corporation was organized to provide insurance to customers in the event of a broker's insolvency.

> In trying to determine who was eligible to receive the $2.74 per share, the *Dole* court first determined that there were 36.8 million issued and outstanding shares of Dole Foods stock. It next examined brokerage records to determine the owners of those 36.8 million shares, and those brokerage records showed there were 49.2 million apparently valid shares of Dole stock.
>
> *What accounted for the extra 12.6 million shares?*
>
> Imprecise records of ownership by brokers and other intermediaries, who had borrowed, lent, sold, and repurchased Dole shares so often, with such shoddy recordkeeping, that it was impossible to precisely determine the true owners of the shares.

The *Dole* case highlights one problem with super negotiability: it allows intermediaries to transfer (buy, sell, borrow or lend) "phantom" securities, i.e., securities the intermediary does not actually own or control. In *Dole*, the phantom securities were the 12.6 million shares that were listed as owned by customers but did not exist.

In response to the criticisms regarding the Uniform Law Commission's decision to give intermediaries super negotiability, the Commission issued a statement claiming that the Model Acts did not require crypto owners to use intermediaries to hold their crypto, but that such use is purely "voluntary." However, in *Forbes*, Andrea Tinianow, a leading UCC and crypto lawyer (and noted "Blockchain Czarina") pointed out that the Model Acts *require* crypto owners to relinquish their property rights to intermediaries if they wish to avail themselves of the UCC's protections. In addition, according to Tinianow, in the absence of an explicit contract, the Model Acts would infer or create a contract between a customer and an intermediary even in circumstances where no contract exists.

To support her argument, Tinianow noted the following language:

> *"To the extent that there is no agreement that complies with [the relevant section], **the relationship between a licensee or registrant and a user is determined as if the licensee or registrant and the user have an agreement** that complies with [the relevant section] and specifies that the [UCC as adopted by the] state governs the agreement."* [Emphasis supplied]

That language indicates that according to the Model Acts, intermediaries would have the same rights that apply in traditional securities markets, opening the door for *Dole*-type issues for crypto held through intermediaries.

What's really going on?

> *The answer to all your questions is money.*
> —Don Ohlmeyer, NBC Executive

At its core, the debate is about the ability of intermediaries to profit from their customers' crypto. In testimony by Uniform Law Commission Commissioner Keith Rowley to the Nevada Senate, Rowley stated that he and his Commission colleagues were concerned about the lack of financing opportunities for intermediaries due to the "the unavailability of fractional reserve banking [for crypto]." In other words, the ability of intermediaries to take risks and earn profits with their customers' crypto.

Fractional reserve banking is a banking practice in which a bank keeps only a fraction of its deposits in reserve and available for immediate withdrawal. The remaining deposits are lent out to borrowers. In simple terms, it is the ability to lend out most deposits and hold back only small percentage, in the hope that most depositors will not ask for their money at the same time. The funds lent out earn interest and allow financial institutions to make a profit. The box below, citing the 1946 Frank Capra film *It's a*

Wonderful Life, provides a practical example of fractional reserve banking.

It's a *Wonderful Life* explains fractional reserve banking

In one of the movie's more famous scenes, George Bailey (played by Jimmy Stewart) confronts a mob of customers demanding their deposits back  from his Bailey Building & Loan community bank, based on fictional situation remarkably similar to the Great Depression.

In the film, Bailey tells the mob that he cannot give them their money immediately because their deposits have been invested in other assets like their and their neighbors' homes and local businesses. As noted by the *Atlantic:*

> *"the movie's plot also touches on some still-relevant financial topics, including the nature of banking, the philosophical calculus behind issuing loans, and the way American families' financial fates are intertwined."*

> —Bourree Lam And Gillian B. White, *The Morality of Banking in It's a Wonderful Life,* The Atlantic (Dec. 23, 2016).

All banks use fractional reserve banking to earn profits. However, to ensure that banks remain solvent, federal banking regulations mandate a required ratio, typically around ten percent of deposits, that must be held in reserve. That ten percent reserve requirement represents a hard limit to the amount of money banks can lend against their deposits.

For non-bank crypto intermediaries, if they had super negotiability, there would be no legal (as opposed to prudential) limit on their ability to borrow or lend a customer's crypto in order to earn profits. The practice of an intermediary using a customer's assets to earn profits, often through borrowing or lending those assets, is called rehypothecation.

Financial intermediaries sometimes rehypothecate more assets than they hold, leading to what is called an uncovered position—one not fully backed by an actual asset.[10] Examples 1 and 2 below demonstrate risks of rehypothecation and uncovered positions in crypto.

Example 1

Assume a crypto financial intermediary (Hazard Co.) holds 100 of Bibi's bitcoins (and no other bitcoin holdings), but decides to lend out 140 bitcoins to Chaun. At that point, Hazard Co. would have a 40-bitcoin uncovered position. This example raises two obvious questions:

1) *How can Hazard Co. lend out more crypto than it holds?*

Good question. The reason is because the 140 bitcoins often never actually have to leave Hazard Co. Think of the average loan: when the loan is made, all that happens is the bank makes a bookkeeping entry that states the borrower has additional funds. But the funds don't necessarily leave the bank. Also, if the borrower uses the funds to pay another of the bank's customers, all that happens is another

---

[10] Much of this section, and the examples provided, is based on Caitlin Long's article, *Two Things That Don't Mix Well: Bitcoin Rehypothecation And Chain Forks*, Forbes (Aug. 21, 2018).

bookkeeping entry, from one bank customer to another.

2) *Why would Hazard Co. want to create an uncovered position?*

Speculation. In our example, Hazard Co. would earn interest from lending out 140 bitcoins to Chaun, even though it had only Bibi's 100 bitcoins. So long as all 140 bitcoins do not leave Hazard Co., this house of cards will stand.

Although creating an uncovered position is risky, it can be very profitable, because it allows financial institutions to earn interest on assets they do not own. The risk, however, falls onto customers who may not be able to get their assets back if a financial institution's risks do not pay off. Taking risks and passing those risks onto others is called "moral hazard." Both rehypothecation and moral hazard were contributing factors to the 2008 financial crisis.[11]

As if the risks of rehypothecation and uncovered positions were not significant enough, the reality is that those risks are more pronounced with crypto because of potential for forks, as described in Example 2 below:

Example 2

Using the facts of Example 1, assume bitcoin forked into two new cryptos (NewBitcoin and Crypto2) during the time it was lent out. Because owners of the pre-forked bitcoin will become owners of both NewBitcoin and Crypto2, Hazard Co. now has doubled its uncovered position. Before the fork, it had a 40-bitcoin uncovered position. After the fork, it would have a 40-NewBitcoin uncovered position and a 40-Crypto2 uncovered position,

---

[11] See Sean Walters, *One Lehman Lesson: The Perils of Rehypothecation*, Wall Street Journal (Sep. 25, 2008).

neither of which Hazard Co. would own. The fork raises two additional problems for Hazard Co.:

1)   Exposure: if both NewBitcoin and Crypto2 are as valuable as the pre-forked crypto (for example, the pre-forked bitcoin was worth $10,000, and immediately after the fork, both NewBitcoin and Crypto2 are each worth $10,000), Hazard Co.'s uncovered exposure would double.

2)   Delivery: after forks, as was the case in the Bitcoin Cash (BCH) November 2018 fork, it has sometimes taken several days before forked coins were traded and listed on crypto exchanges. Once listed, the prices of the post-forked coins often fluctuate wildly. If Chaun wanted her 40 units of NewBitcoin and 40 units of Crypto 2 immediately, Hazard Co. would be forced to acquire 40 units of both NewBitcoin and Crypto2 at a time when the market is illiquid and the prices are volatile. Also, to make matters worse for Hazard Co., Bibi could demand that Hazard Co. return her 100-units of both NewBitcoin and Crypto 2.

To avoid these problems, many in the crypto community propose preventing rehypothecation by requiring 100 percent collateralization of crypto absent specific authorization from customers to rehypothecate.

State Law: A Tale of Two States

In the US, state crypto regulations are all over the map (pun intended). Some states have issued detailed guidance on crypto, while others have been mostly silent, relying on existing laws and rules. Two states, Wyoming and New York, however, have enacted comprehensive regimes with far different reactions from the crypto community:

- Wyoming has received an overwhelmingly positive reaction that has resulted in a number of crypto businesses choosing to relocate there; and

- New York has received a less-than-enthusiastic reaction that has resulted in a number of crypto businesses leaving the state.

Wyoming

Wyoming has passed an array of laws that seek to clarify and encourage crypto businesses, in hopes to become the "Delaware of digital asset law," a reference to Delaware's dominance in corporate law. Wyoming's laws divide blockchain-based assets into three categories:

1) Digital Securities: crypto that would be deemed securities under existing US law and would be recognized as securities under the UCC;

2) Digital Consumer Assets: utility tokens or crypto that function as something other than as a currency, and would be recognized as general intangibles under the UCC; and

3) Virtual Currencies: crypto that function primarily as money and would be recognized as money under the UCC.

Wyoming's taxonomy attempts to provide clarity to businesses regarding how Wyoming law will treat different types of crypto. The following are some of the provisions that have drawn the most attention and support from the crypto community:

- Classifies digital assets (crypto) as property within the context of the UCC, which means individuals and businesses have the right to own digital assets without the need for intermediaries. This contradicts the approach of the Model Acts, which gave intermediaries preference with respect to ownership.

- Allows securities to be issued in tokenized form, which will allow any business, not just crypto businesses, to issue securities directly on a blockchain.

- Permits the creation of special purpose depository institutions to serve blockchain businesses.

- Specifies a control-based method of perfecting security interests in digital assets, and provides that a transferee of a digital asset takes the asset free of any security interest two years after the transferee takes the asset for value, absent notice of an adverse claim.

- Authorizes banks to provide custodial services for digital assets consistent with the SEC's qualified custodian requirements.

- Creates a regulatory safe space for FinTech companies (a FinTech sandbox)[12] to test innovative financial products or services by:

---

[12] A FinTech sandbox refers to a regulatory framework for FinTech companies and products that provides a regulatory environment that fosters innovative financial products and activities, and allows for smaller-scale, live testing of innovation under special regulatory exemptions, allowances, or other limited, time-bound exceptions. Broadly, regulatory sandboxes allow businesses to test non-traditional products under the regulator's supervision with less risk of punishment. To operate in the sandbox, regulators require businesses to incorporate protections to insulate customers and the broader market from risks of their non-traditional products. The concept of a regulatory sandbox developed soon after the 2008 financial crisis as an attempt to

o   allowing regulators to waive rules relating to banking, corporate law, electronic records, consumer credit, and money transmission; and

o   specifying that FinTech products or services can be tested in the sandbox for up to three years.

New York

New York's regulatory regime for crypto was developed by the New York State Department of Financial Services (NYDFS). Under that regime, companies that want to conduct crypto business activities are required to obtain a license, called a BitLicense, from NYDFS. The BitLicense regulations were finalized in June 2015 and became effective August 8, 2015.

According to the NYDFS, the goals of the BitLicense regime are to prevent money laundering, protect consumers, and establish cybersecurity rules and procedures. The BitLicense regime applies to individuals and business entities that live or operate in New York that transmit, hold, buy, sell, administer, or issue crypto as a consumer business or crypto exchange, but does not apply to businesses that simply accept crypto as payment.

In general, the BitLicense regime sets forth rules for the use, control, administration, maintenance, storage, custody, issuance, and exchange of crypto, as well as rules for crypto-related software development. It also imposes strict consumer protection and disclosure requirements for businesses offering crypto-related services. To obtain a BitLicense, a business must pay a $5,000 application fee and file a thirty-page application, and estimates are that the cost of gathering the required information can exceed $100,000.

---

address the frictions between businesses' desire to innovate and regulators' caution in approving innovative products.

As of December 2019, only 24 companies had been granted BitLicenses, and some companies reported having to wait nearly three years for approval. In response to the BitLicense regime, a number of crypto companies have prohibited New York residents from using their services, and the crypto exchanges BitFinex, ShapeShift, and Kraken publicly pulled their businesses out of New York to avoid the BitLicense process. According to Jesse Powell, the CEO of Kraken, BitLicense would have forced Kraken to "disclose all the information about our entire global client base to the state of New York," which was "potentially illegal" under the privacy laws of other countries.[13]

One argument offered in favor of the heightened New York requirements is that because New York serves as a global financial hub, it needs a more rigorous regulatory regime to maintain the integrity of global financial markets. Martin Weiss, the founder of Weiss Cryptocurrency Ratings, neatly sums up the New York position regarding the BitLicense regime:

> "Cryptocurrencies are, in essence, borderless. Regulation, in order to catch up, would also have to be borderless, crossing not only state boundaries but also national boundaries. New York is in a unique situation because it regulates a major financial center, the largest in the world. So as long as all those corporations want to remain domiciled in New York, legislators in Albany do have a jurisdictional reach that sticks. In most places in the world, if you try to regulate cryptocurrencies, they'll just move to another jurisdiction. That is bound to happen with most of cryptocurrency institutions. But that's not the case with New York."[14]

---

[13] Remarks of Jesse Powell, 2018 Consensus conference (May 21, 2018).

[14] See Kirill Bryanov, *Blockchain and the City: New York State as a "Tough" Model of Crypto Regulation,* Cointelegraph (Feb. 21, 2019).

In late 2019, NYDFS announced it intended to update its BitLicense regulations early in 2020. As part of the announcement, NYDFS published and sought comments on two proposed coin adoption or listing options:

1) a proposal to provide a NYDFS-approved list of all coins that are allowed for virtual currency business activities without the prior approval by the authority, and

2) a model framework for listing coins, which would enable licensees to self-certify the listing or adoption of new coins.

Securities Laws and the SEC

One of the most contentious issues in crypto has been determining whether certain crypto are securities, thus subject to federal securities regulation. The answer to that question has far-reaching implications for the sale, tradability, and ultimately the utility of crypto both in the US and abroad.

Crypto designated as securities are subject to myriad laws and regulations in the US, providing some measure of safety to investors. However, a security designation also raises the costs and risks associated with bringing that crypto to market, thereby implicitly encouraging crypto companies to operate in more crypto-friendly jurisdictions. If the US cannot strike a fair balance between investor protection and supporting crypto businesses, it risks losing generations of crypto businesses to the rest of the world.

Introduction to Securities Laws and Regulations

For readers unfamiliar with securities regulation, the questions and answers below provide some important definitions, as well as a brief history of US securities laws.

What is a security?

In lay terms, a security is a tradeable financial asset whose value is derived from an ownership right or a contractual claim. Financial assets include stock and other equity instruments, debt instruments, and bank deposits. In general, tangible assets like land, cars, commodities, or racehorses are not considered financial assets; however, contractual claims based on the value of any of those tangible assets would be considered financial assets.

When were federal securities laws first passed?

In the US, federal securities laws date back to the early 1930s. President Franklin D. Roosevelt signed the Securities Act of 1933

('33 Act or Securities Act) as part of the New Deal. The '33 Act governed issuances of securities and was followed the next year by the Securities Exchange Act of 1934 ('34 Act or Exchange Act), which governed exchanges and trading of securities.

Why did Congress pass the securities laws?

The stock market crash of 1929. Prior to the crash, securities markets were loosely regulated by individual states, not the federal government. Those state markets boomed during the 1920s, fueled by a new tech sector that introduced radio, movies, bulldozers, frozen food, penicillin, and electric razors.

Between 1925 and 1929, that hot tech sector fueled a 300 percent increase in overall stock prices. Unfortunately for retail investors, however, much of the information available to them was fraudulent. Scammers and criminals like Joseph P. Kennedy (whose son would later become president) used nefarious schemes, such as pump-and-dumps and wash sales, to mislead investors.[15]

After the crash, Congress launched a number of investigations that revealed:

- widespread efforts to manipulate securities markets, including payoffs to journalists and politicians;

- rampant insider trading by corporate officers and directors;

- corrupt practices by corporate insiders, including paying themselves exorbitant salaries and giving themselves interest-free loans; and

- investment banks tipping politicians and corporate executives about upcoming deals, allowing them to

---

[15] See SEC Historical Society, *431 Days: Joseph P. Kennedy and the Creation of the SEC* (1934-35).

invest before the public and profit once the securities started trading.

Twenty-five days after taking office, President Roosevelt urged Congress to pass a law that would "put the burden of telling the whole truth" on sellers of securities. Two months later, the '33 Act was signed into law.

Who administers the securities laws?

Initially, the '33 Act was administered by the Federal Trade Commission and was limited to regulating new stock issuances. However, it soon became clear to Congress and the Roosevelt administration that stronger laws and enforcement were needed. The next year, Congress and the President strengthened the nation's securities laws by:

- enacting the '34 Act, which broadened US securities laws to cover not only securities issuances, but also securities trading; and

- creating the Securities and Exchange Commission (SEC), to serve as an independent agency to administer the securities laws.

Federal securities regulations, then and now, have two primary goals:

1) encourage companies to disclose accurate financial information to investors so investors can make informed decisions; and

2) establish laws and penalties for fraud and misrepresentation in securities markets.

The SEC enforces the securities laws to ensure that companies offering securities for sale to the public provide accurate disclosures about the companies' business, the securities offered, and the risks involved in investing in those securities. In addition, the SEC provides rules to ensure that those who sell and trade securities—brokers, dealers, and exchanges—treat investors fairly and honestly.

One of the most powerful weapons in the SEC's arsenal is Section 10(b) of the '34 Act, which prohibits "any manipulative or deceptive device or contrivance in contravention of such rules and regulations as the Commission may prescribe as necessary or appropriate in the public interest or for the protection of investors." The latter part of that quote, "as the Commissioner may prescribe. . ." gives the SEC the power to issue rules and regulations regarding the best way to enforce Section 10(b), and provides the statutory basis for the SEC's most powerful anti-fraud weapon, Rule 10b-5.

Adopted in 1942, Rule 10b-5 makes it illegal to:

a)   employ any device, scheme, or artifice to defraud;

b)   make any untrue statement of a material fact or to omit a material fact necessary in order to make the statements made, in light of the circumstances under which they were made, not misleading; or

c)   engage in any act, practice, or course of business which operates or would operate as a fraud or deceit upon any person, in connection with the purchase or sale of any security.

Under US law, the definition of a security (restated in its entirety below) is extremely long and intended to cover many different types of financial arrangements. For the purposes of this book and crypto, however, the critical terms are underlined:

The term "security" means, (unless the context otherwise requires) any note, stock, treasury stock, security future, security-based swap, bond, debenture, evidence of indebtedness, certificate of interest or participation in any profit-sharing agreement, collateral-trust certificate, preorganization certificate or subscription, transferable share, <u>investment contract</u>, voting-trust certificate, certificate of deposit for a security, fractional undivided interest in oil, gas, or other mineral rights, any put, call, straddle, option, or privilege on any security, certificate of deposit, or group or index of securities (including any interest therein or based on the value thereof), or any put, call, straddle, option, or privilege entered into on a national securities exchange relating to foreign currency, or, in general, any interest or instrument commonly known as a "security", or any certificate of interest or participation in, temporary or interim certificate for, receipt for, guarantee of, or warrant or right to subscribe to or purchase, any of the foregoing.

An investment contract is a catch-all term that serves as the basis for the SEC's exercise of jurisdiction over certain crypto. The term was largely undefined until the 1946 US Supreme Court case of *SEC v. W.J. Howey Co.* (*Howey*), which created a four-element test to determine whether a financial asset would be considered a security.

In *Howey*, the Court defined an investment contract as:

> *"a contract, transaction or scheme whereby a person invests his money in a common enterprise and is led to expect profits solely from the efforts of the promoter or a third party."*

That language came to be known as the *Howey* test, and as it is currently understood, treats a transaction as an investment contract—thus as a security—whenever there is:

1)   an investment of money or other property;

2)   in a "common enterprise;"

3) with an expectation of profits from the investment; and

4) the expectation of profits is based mostly on the efforts of others.

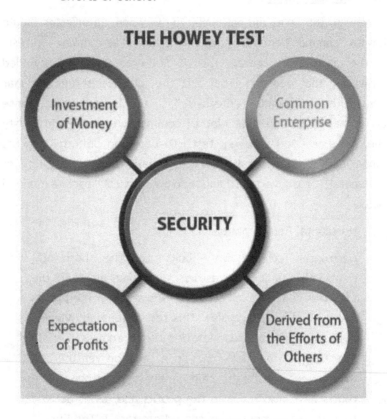

THE HOWEY TEST

Investment of Money

Common Enterprise

SECURITY

Expectation of Profits

Derived from the Efforts of Others

Graphic courtesy of Congressional Research Service

Each element is discussed below.

1) Investment of Money

This is the simplest element of the *Howey* test. The language in *Howey* required the investment to be made in "money," but later court decisions expanded the definition to include other types of property. To evaluate this element, courts look to see whether the investor gives up "some tangible and definable [property] in return for an interest that had substantially the characteristics of a security."[16]

2) Common Enterprise

In *Howey,* the Court did not specify with whom an investor should have a "common" enterprise, akin to a shared or common interest. In the years since *Howey,* the US Supreme Court has avoided answering that question. That left the job of determining what constituted a "common enterprise" to the lower courts. Those courts had to decide what type of common interest would satisfy the Supreme Court's *Howey* test. To date, no uniformity exists among courts, but three distinct commonality tests have emerged: horizontal, broad vertical, and narrow vertical, each explained below.

Horizontal Commonality

Horizontal commonality looks to the horizontal relationship among investors, analyzing whether the investors pool their investments and share in the profits and risks of the enterprise. This test is generally viewed as the most difficult to meet, because it requires multiple investors pooling their funds in a common venture and focuses on the relationship amongst investors. Some courts have also required the profits and losses derived from the investment to be shared pro-rata.[17] The First,[18]

---

[16]   See *International Brotherhood of Teamsters v. Daniel,* 439 U.S. 551 (1979).

[17]   See, e.g., *Stenger v. R.H. Love Galleries, Inc.,* 741 F.2d 144, 146 (7th Cir. 1984); *SEC v. Banner Fund Int'l,* 211 F.3d 602, 614 (D.C. Cir. 2000).

[18]   See *SEC & Exch. Comm'n v. SG Ltd.,* 265 F.3d 42 (1st Cir. 2001).

Second,[19] Third,[20] Fourth,[21] Sixth,[22] Seventh,[23] Ninth,[24] and D.C.[25] Circuit Courts of Appeal (Circuits) accept horizontal commonality, and some of those courts have yet to rule on whether they will accept other types of commonality.

Vertical Commonality

Vertical commonality looks to the vertical relationship between investors and promoters, analyzing the extent to which investors are dependent on the promoter's efforts or expertise. Courts differ on what is needed to show vertical commonality:

Broad Vertical Commonality

Some courts require the investors' fortunes to be related to the promoter's efforts or expertise. In such cases, so long as the investors rely on the promoter's efforts or expertise, there will be broad vertical commonality. This is generally regarded as the easiest to satisfy. Both the Fifth[26] and Eleventh[27] Circuits require broad vertical commonality.

---

[19] See *Revak v. Realty Corp.*, 18 F.3d 81, 87 (2d Cir. 1994).

[20] See *Salcer v. Merrill Lynch*, 682 F.2d 459, 460 (3d Cir. 1982) (adopting horizontal commonality).

[21] See *Teague v. Bakker*, 35 F.3d 978 (4th Cir. 1994).

[22] See *Curran v. Merrill Lynch*, 622 F.2d 216, 222 (6th Cir. 1980) (dispensing with vertical commonality in favor of horizontal commonality).

[23] See *Milnarik v. M-S Commodities*, 457 F.2d at 274, 276-77 (7th Cir. 1972).

[24] See *Hocking v. Dubois*, 885 F.2d 1449, 1459 (9th Cir.1989) (en banc).

[25] See *SEC v. Banner Fund Intern.*, 211 F.3d 602, 341 (D.C. Cir. 2000).

[26] See *SEC v. Cont'l Commodities Corp.*, 497 F.2d 516, 516 (5th Cir. 1974).

[27] See *Messer v. E.F. Hutton & Co.*, 833 F.2d 909, 915 (11th Cir. 1987). Although the court focused its holding on the efforts of the promoter under the fourth prong of *Howey*, the court nonetheless cited a Fifth Circuit case to help guide its decision.

<u>Narrow Vertical Commonality</u>

Others courts require the investors' fortunes to be linked to the promoter's fortunes. In such cases, if the promoter profits when the investors profit, there will be narrow vertical commonality. However, if the promoter earns a fixed fee or a commission that is not dependent on the profitability of the enterprise, it is unlikely a court will find narrow vertical commonality. Only the Ninth Circuit accepts narrow vertical commonality,[28] but in the past, the Ninth Circuit has also accepted horizontal commonality.[29]

As discussed later in the chapter, the SEC's position on commonality for crypto appears to be "any commonality will suffice."

3)   Expectation of Profits

This element looks to whether there is a reasonable expectation of profits from the investment, and whether that expectation is the principal motivation for the investment. In determining what are considered "profits," courts have focused primarily on capital appreciation or earnings of the enterprise. Importantly, the Supreme Court has held that "when a purchaser is motivated by a desire to *use or consume* the item purchased . . . the securities laws do not apply."[30] [Emphasis supplied]

That "use or consume" exception, widely described as "utility," is often relied upon by crypto issuers claiming their tokens are not securities. However, the SEC has emphasized that simply labeling a token a "utility token" does not magically exempt the token from

---

[28] But see *Hocking v. Dubois*, 839 F.2d 560, 567 (9th Cir. 1988) (stipulating that the Ninth Circuit Court of Appeals has endorsed strict vertical commonality, but not to the full exclusion of horizontal commonality).

[29] See *Hocking v. Dubois*, 885 F.2d 1449, 1459 (9th Cir.1989) (rehearing en banc).

[30] *Howey* at 300.

securities laws. To date, the SEC has not provided a clear answer on exactly how much utility a token needs to avoid being deemed a security, but has offered guidance (described later in this chapter) to narrow the inquiry.

4) Based on Efforts of Others

Howey's fourth element requires that the expectation of profits from the investment be based on "the efforts of others." The original language from *Howey* stated that the profits were based "solely" on the efforts of others, but the "solely" requirement has been relaxed by most courts. Today, the relevant inquiry is "whether the efforts made by those other than the investor are the undeniably significant ones, those essential managerial efforts which affect the failure or success of the enterprise."[31]

Under US law, all offers and sales of securities must either be registered under the securities laws or have qualified for an exemption from registration. To register a security, an issuer must disclose to potential investors detailed information about the investment, including a description of the business and its management, the security to be offered, and certified financial statements. According to the accounting and consulting firm PWC, the costs of the registration process for an initial public offering (IPO), which often requires the involvement of lawyers, accountants and bankers, typically exceed $1 million.

The SEC and Crypto

Prior to 2017, the SEC had not taken a public position on whether crypto were securities. On July 25, 2017, following a hack on a crypto hedge fund called "The DAO," the SEC made its position clear

---

[31] *SEC v. Glenn W. Turner Enterprises, Inc.*, 474 F.2d 476, 482 (9th Cir. 1973); *United Housing Foundation, Inc. v. Forman*, 421 U.S. 837 (1975).

when it issued The DAO Report, excerpted below, announcing its position that all crypto that met the *Howey* test were securities.

U.S. SECURITIES AND EXCHANGE COMMISSION

SEC Issues Investigative Report Concluding DAO Tokens, a Digital Asset, Were Securities

U.S. Securities Laws May Apply to Offers, Sales, and Trading of Interests in Virtual Organizations

THE DAO REPORT

(the information below is based on The DAO Report)

The DAO was an example of a Decentralized Autonomous Organization, a term used to describe a "virtual" organization embodied in computer code and executed on a distributed ledger or blockchain. The DAO was created by a company called Slock.it and its co-founders, with the objective of operating as a virtual hedge fund. The DAO would generate assets through the sale of DAO Tokens to investors, and those assets would then be used to fund investment projects. The holders of DAO Tokens, as a return on their investment, would share in the earnings generated from the projects. In addition, DAO Token holders would be able to re-sell their DAO Tokens.

In 2016, The DAO launched and raised over $150 million worth of ETH from the sale of DAO Tokens. However, before The DAO was able to commence funding projects, an attacker used a flaw in The DAO's code to steal approximately one-third of the ETH raised. The stolen ETH was valued at between $50-$60 million.

The SEC launched an investigation into The DAO hack, and as part of its investigation, considered (i) the threshold question of whether DAO Tokens were securities, and (ii) whether US securities laws applied to the offer and sale of DAO Tokens. Based on its investigation, the SEC issued The DAO Report, determining that DAO Tokens were securities, and the offer and sale of DAO Tokens constituted an offering of securities.

The DAO Report, issued in July 2017, marked the unofficial beginning of the battle between the crypto community and the SEC. In the following years, a primary point of contention became how the SEC would determine whether a certain crypto was a security. Many in the crypto community called on the SEC to issue clear rules for determining how the unique features of crypto would influence the SEC's investment contract (*Howey*) analysis.

After The DAO Report was issued, some crypto companies moved offshore to avoid US securities regulations. Many in the crypto community complained that the SEC's lack of clarity was a motivating factor. To provide more clarity, in April 2019, the SEC published the *Framework for "Investment Contract" Analysis of Digital Assets* (Framework) to help market participants understand how the SEC would determine whether a particular crypto would be considered a security. Although the guidance was welcomed, it came with one important caveat: it was not binding. The Framework included the following cautionary language:

> This framework represents [the SEC] Staff views and is not a rule, regulation, or statement of the Commission. The Commission has neither approved nor disapproved its content. This framework, like other Staff guidance, is not binding on [SEC] Divisions or the Commission. It does not constitute legal advice, for which you should consult with

your own attorney. It does not modify or replace any existing applicable laws, regulations, or rules.

Despite its cautionary language, the Framework provided useful guidance regarding how the SEC would determine whether a token was a security, and laid out the SEC's three-element[32] *Howey* test:

1) Investment of Money;

2) Common Enterprise; and

3) Reasonable Expectation of Profits Derived from Efforts of Others.

The Framework's analysis is below.

1)   Investment of Money

The Framework provides that this element is "typically satisfied in an offer and sale of a digital asset because the digital asset is purchased or otherwise acquired in exchange for value, whether in the form of real (or fiat) currency, another digital asset, or other type of consideration." In a footnote, however, the Framework discussed airdrops, which are free distributions of crypto tokens to holders of other crypto typically used to promote circulation of the airdropped crypto.[33]

The footnote noted that if the airdropped tokens were issued "in exchange for services [by the recipients] designed to advance the issuer's economic interests and foster a trading market for its securities," then the investment of money element would likely be satisfied. The SEC's position on airdrops mirrors its position on "free

---

[32]   The Framework collapsed the final two elements into one, but in its analysis, separates them again.

[33]   See Framework, footnote 9.

stock" scams that operated in the late 1990s. According to then-SEC Enforcement Dir. Richard H. Walker:

> *"Free stock is really a misnomer in these cases. While cash did not change hands, the companies that issued the stock received valuable benefits. Under these circumstances, the securities laws entitle investors to full and fair disclosure, which they did not receive in these cases."*[34]

2)   Common Enterprise

The Framework's common enterprise analysis consisted of a one-sentence conclusion:

> *"In evaluating digital assets, we (the SEC) have found that a 'common enterprise' typically exists."*

That conclusory analysis included a footnote (Footnote 11), noting that based on the SEC's analysis, "investments in digital assets have constituted investments in a common enterprise because the fortunes of digital asset purchasers have been linked to each other *or* to the success of the promoter's efforts." [Emphasis supplied]

In other words, the SEC appears to take the position that it does not matter what type of commonality exists. That conclusion is based on the language of Footnote 11, which covers:

- the horizontal test through the use of the language, "the fortunes of digital asset purchasers have been linked to each other;" and

- the vertical tests through the use of the language, "the fortunes of digital asset

---

[34]   See SEC Press Release 99-83 (Jul. 22, 1999).

> purchasers have been 'linked to' . . . the success of the promoter's efforts," which would satisfy the more difficult narrow vertical test as well as the less stringent broad vertical test.

The SEC's commonality position has been criticized by many in the crypto industry, because what the SEC appears to be saying is:

> *We will generally treat a token as satisfying our common enterprise test so long as it satisfies any commonality test.*

Whether a court would agree with such a loose definition of commonality has yet to be determined, and is among the issues litigated in *SEC v. Kik Interactive, Inc.* (*Kik*), described later in the chapter. The *Kik* case is widely regarded as the most important test case for securities regulation of crypto.

3)   Reasonable Expectation of Profits Derived from Efforts of Others

After joining the final two *Howey* elements, the Framework then separates them into (i) reliance on the efforts of others, and (ii) reasonable expectation of profits. Mirroring the Framework, those are discussed below in an abbreviated form.

(i)   *Reliance on the Efforts of Others*

In evaluating this element, the Framework focuses on the role of what the SEC calls an "Active Participant" (AP), defined as the promoter, sponsor, or other party:

> *"responsible for the development, improvement (or enhancement), operation, or*

promotion of the network, particularly if purchasers of the digital asset expect an AP to be performing or overseeing tasks that are necessary for the network or digital asset to achieve or retain its intended purpose or functionality."

The Framework then identifies two key issues in its "efforts of others" analysis:

1. Does the purchaser reasonably expect to rely on the efforts of an AP?

2. Are the AP's efforts the undeniably significant ones, those essential managerial efforts which affect the failure or success of the enterprise, as opposed to efforts that are more ministerial in nature?

Because many crypto tokens are on decentralized blockchains, the Framework provides examples in which this element will be satisfied, including situations in which:

- essential managerial tasks or responsibilities are to be performed by an AP rather than an unaffiliated, dispersed community of network users;

- an AP creates or supports a market for, or the price of, the digital asset;

- an AP has a lead or central role in the direction of the ongoing development of the network or the digital asset including governance issues, code updates, or how transactions are validated;

- an AP has a continuing managerial role in making decisions about or exercising judgment concerning the network or the characteristics or rights the digital asset represents; and

- purchasers would reasonably expect the AP to undertake efforts to promote its own interests and enhance the value of the network or digital asset.

According to the Framework, while none of the characteristics are determinative, the stronger their presence, the more likely it is that the SEC will determine a purchaser is relying on the efforts of others. Many have complained that the Framework provides little in the way of actual guidance about what the SEC views as the most, or even more, important factors.

(ii) *Reasonable Expectation of Profits*

The Framework generally acknowledges that profits can result from capital appreciation or earnings, but adds that price appreciation resulting solely from external market forces (such as general inflationary trends or the economy) impacting the supply and demand for an underlying asset generally would not be considered profits under *Howey*.

The Framework then lists a number of characteristics (too long to reproduce here) that would make it more likely there would be a reasonable expectation of profits. The Framework also identified factors weighing against a finding that digital asset purchasers have a reasonable expectation of profits, including whether purchasers are buying the assets for consumptive or utility purposes.

Other Framework guidance

The Framework also provides guidance on the circumstances under which a particular crypto would no longer be considered a security. The SEC acknowledged that crypto previously sold as a security may not always be considered a security, and would examine the following factors in making its determination:

- Purchasers of the digital asset no longer reasonably expect that continued development efforts of an AP will be a key factor for determining the value of the digital asset.

- The value of the digital asset has shown a direct and stable correlation to the value of the good or service for which it may be exchanged or redeemed.

- The trading volume for the digital asset corresponds to the level of demand for the good or service for which it may be exchanged or redeemed.

- Whether holders are able to use the digital asset for its intended functionality, such as to acquire goods and services on or through the network or platform.

- Whether any economic benefit that may be derived from appreciation in the value of the digital asset is incidental to obtaining the right to use it for its intended functionality.

- No AP has access to material, non-public information or could otherwise be deemed to hold material inside information about the digital asset.

A new proposal

In a February 2020 speech, SEC Commissioner Hester Peirce, known in the crypto community as "Crypto Mom," proposed a safe harbor for crypto projects looking to raise funds. Peirce stated the proposal was necessary "to achieve the investor protection objectives of the securities laws, as well as the need to provide the regulatory flexibility that allows innovation to flourish."[35]

Peirce detailed her proposal, which she admitted was a work-in-progress, in an appendix to her speech that was made available on the SEC's website.[36] According to Peirce's proposal:

> This safe harbor is intended to provide Initial Development Teams with a three-year time period within which they can facilitate participation in, and the development of, a functional or decentralized network, exempt from the registration provisions of the federal securities laws so long as the conditions are met. The safe harbor is also designed to protect token purchasers by requiring disclosures tailored to the needs of the purchasers and preserving the application of the anti-fraud provisions of the federal securities laws.
>
> Upon the conclusion of the three-year period, the Initial Development Team must determine whether token transactions involve the offer or sale of a security. Token transactions may not constitute securities transactions if the network has matured to a functioning or decentralized network. The definition of Network Maturity is intended to provide clarity as to when a token transaction should no longer be considered a security

---

[35] Hester M. Peirce, SEC Commissioner, *Running on Empty: A Proposal to Fill the Gap Between Regulation and Decentralization*, speech at International Blockchain Congress (Feb. 6, 2020).

[36] See www.sec.gov/news/speech/peirce-remarks-blockress-2020-02-06.

transaction but, as always, the analysis will require an evaluation of the particular facts and circumstances.

Peirce's proposed safe harbor has been generally well-received by the crypto community.

Securities Laws and Token Offerings

Most crypto has historically been offered to investors through Initial Coin Offerings (ICOs). An ICO is a smart contract that executes a public sale of crypto tokens. ICOs are similar to IPOs in most respects, except:

1) ICOs are offered on a blockchain;

2) ICOs are offered through smart contracts;

3) ICOs are generally used for underfunded development projects that need money to move forward to completion; and

4) crypto tokens issued in an ICO are distributed directly to investors' accounts (crypto wallets), but generally are not immediately tradable on an exchange.

The market for ICOs was huge in 2017 and 2018, with over 3,000 ICOs and $6.2 and $7.8 billion raised respectively each year.[37] That market cooled in 2019, with end-of-year totals of just over $370 million.

Because ICO tokens are held in individual crypto wallets, there was often no readily-accessible market to trade those tokens after the ICO, leaving many investors without a means to sell them. In order to provide a market for their tokens, many ICO projects sought to have their tokens listed on an exchange. Despite their efforts,

---

[37] ICO data from icodata.io.

roughly 90 percent of ICO projects were never listed on an exchange.

One market response to the ICO token listing problem was the introduction of Initial Exchange Offerings (IEOs), which are similar to ICOs in all but one respect: IEO tokens are not issued to individual crypto wallets, but instead are listed and immediately tradable on an exchange. That allows investors to purchase IEO tokens through their existing exchange accounts, and simplifies the fundraising details for issuers. Other benefits touted by IEO proponents include:

Investor Protection

Because exchanges put their reputations on the line in listing IEO tokens, exchanges are incentivized to ensure that only reputable projects are listed. As a result, exchanges would likely be viewed as having a duty to their stakeholders to perform enough due diligence to ensure each project they list is legitimate.

Tradability and Efficiency

Because investors can purchase tokens directly on the exchange, investors are assured that the tokens will be tradeable. Thus, developers and APs can focus more on the project and less on the fundraising and listing details.

Price Transparency

Many IEOs are structured so that the price of IEO tokens are publicly announced prior to the token being listed, and that price remains fixed during the IEO. That transparency eliminates the wild price speculation that often accompanied ICOs.

Although IEOs provide advantages to ICOs for investors, according to the SEC, exchanges that facilitate IEOs may be breaking US securities laws. At the May 2019 Consensus Conference in New York, the SEC's senior advisor for digital assets and innovation, Valerie Szczepanik, stated that cryptocurrency exchanges that facilitate token sales to US customers likely meet the legal definition of securities dealers, meaning they must follow SEC registration and licensing requirements. Szczepanik added that:

> *"If they are not registered, they will find themselves in trouble in the US if they have a US issuer or US buyers, [or] if they are operating on the US market."*

SEC Enforcement

After The DAO Report was issued, the SEC began to take a more aggressive enforcement position against entities that had offered what it deemed were unregistered securities. Since 2017, the SEC has issued several cease-and-desist to ICO issuers for offering unregistered securities, and many crypto projects have either abandoned their offerings in the US, or placed limits on US users to avoid SEC scrutiny. For example:

The Basis Stablecoin

 In December 2018, the organizers of the Basis stablecoin project abandoned their project and returned $133 million raised from investors, including Google Ventures, Bain Capital Ventures, and Andreessen Horowitz. The organizers took those actions after extended talks with the SEC led the organizers to conclude there was no way to launch their ICO without violating the securities laws. On their website (ww.basis.io), the organizers stated,

> *As regulatory guidance started to trickle out over time, our lawyers came to a consensus that there would be no way to avoid securities status for bond and share tokens and having to apply US securities*

regulation to the system had a serious negative impact on our ability to launch.

The Poloniex Exchange

In May 2019, the crypto exchange Poloniex announced it would "geofence" (prohibit activities of customers in a certain jurisdiction) nine crypto tokens due to regulatory uncertainty regarding whether the SEC would deem those tokens securities under US law. In explaining its action, the company wrote:

> *Specifically, it is not possible to be certain whether US regulators will consider these assets to be securities. We understand how frustrating this choice is for our customers, and for the crypto community more broadly. We believe in the power and potential of these assets, and will continue to focus time and energy on supporting positive policy and regulatory developments for crypto assets in the US and around the world.*

The *Kik* litigation

The most comprehensive exploration of the SEC's and the crypto industry's respective positions can be found by reviewing the SEC's litigation against Kik Interactive, Inc., *SEC v. Kik Interactive.*[38] Kik is a social media messaging company, that, along with its Kin Ecosystem Foundation (Kin), launched a token (the Kin token) based on Kik's messaging app. In June 2019, the SEC filed a complaint alleging Kik conducted an illegal $100 million token offering.

---

[38] *Securities and Exchange Commission v. Kik Interactive*, No. 19-cv-5244 (S.D.N.Y., filed Jun. 4, 2018)

The *Kik* case is widely regarded as a test case of the SEC's position on crypto, for two reasons:

1) Kik effectively invited the SEC to sue by publicly replying to the SEC's inquiries (called a *Wells* Response);[39] and

2) Kik launched a campaign aimed at creating a new *Howey* test for crypto, and organized a website (www.defendcrypto.org) to crowdfund not only its lawsuit against the SEC, but also to assist other crypto firms squaring off against the SEC.

According to one of their lawyers, among the reasons Kik chose to be a test was that:

in the absence of the SEC giving appropriate and clear guidance itself, this is really the only option, . . . we certainly would have preferred for the SEC to have laid out clear guidelines and guidelines that are consistent with the limits of their statutory authority. They haven't done that and so this is really the only way we can see to get to that clarity and to get to the right result, but it will take some time.

—Patrick Gibbs, Attorney for Kik, *Unchained Podcast* (May 28, 2019)

An overview of the significant facts and events in the *Kik* case is below:

- In August 2017, Kik raised over $100 million in an ICO, weeks after the SEC had issued a statement warning that "virtual coins or tokens may be

---

[39] The procedures related to responding to SEC enforcement actions is called a "*Wells*" Process, and a response to a proposed SEC enforcement action is called a "*Wells*" Response." In almost all cases, entities making *Wells* Responses do not make them public.

securities," but offering no actual guidance on how such a determination should be made.

- In November 2017, the SEC notified Kik that it was considering pursuing it for violating US securities laws in its ICO.

- In December 2018, Kik & Kin made public their *Wells* Response to the SEC, alleging that an enforcement action was unwarranted. That submission argued, among other things, that:

  (1) Kin was a currency, thus should not be considered a security; and

  (2) Kin tokens were not investment contracts because:

    i) there was no "common enterprise," between Kik and Kin purchasers;

    ii) there was no expectation of profits because Kin was sold based on its utility; and/or

    iii) to the extent purchasers expected profits, those expectations were not based on the entrepreneurial or management efforts of Kik.

- In May 2019, Kik and Kin launched www.defend crypto.org.

- In June 2019, the SEC sued Kik for conducting an illegal $100 million securities offering.

- In August 2019, Kik filed what was widely regarded as a comprehensive and strategic answer to the SEC complaint, for the reasons set forth below:

Comprehensive

Instead of formally responding to the complaint by giving general denials of the SEC's allegations (which is typical in securities litigation), Kik provided a detailed rebuttal of all the disputed facts and legal issues in SEC's complaint.

Strategic

Kik's answer set the stage for quickly moving the litigation to an appeals court. Generally in securities litigation, a defendant first files a motion to dismiss the lawsuit, which gives the defendant more time to prepare and could force the government to provide more information. Kik forwent the motion to dismiss, and by providing a detailed rebuttal to the SEC's complaint, made it more likely the case would proceed to trial without significant delay. No matter what happens in the trial court, this case will likely be appealed. Kik's answer was designed to move the case to the appeals court, and potentially the US Supreme Court, as expeditiously as possible.

Discovery in the case is expected to be completed in mid-2020, setting the stage for trial later in the year.

Other SEC Action

Around the same time the SEC released the Framework, it also issued its first "No Action Letter" (see box below) with respect to crypto, finding that the ICO tokens issued by Turnkey Jet, Inc. (TKJ) would not be considered securities. TKJ sought to issue fixed-price tokens that would allow token holders to use the TKJ jets as an air charter and air taxi service. The TKJ tokens would be issued on a private blockchain controlled by TKJ.

SEC No Action Letters

Individual or entities uncertain about whether their actions would violate federal securities law may request "No Action" letters from the SEC. Most No Action Letters describe the request, analyze the facts and circumstances involved, and discuss applicable laws and rules. A No Action Letter is considered akin to an SEC stamp of approval.

It took the SEC almost a year to issue the TKJ No Action Letter, a long time considering some No Action Letters have been issued less than one week after requested. The TKJ No Action Letter provided an example of a digital asset that could be offered and sold for use or consumption without implicating securities law registration requirements.

The importance of the TKJ No Action Letter is limited, however, because it addressed only a narrow set of facts i.e., a permissioned, centralized blockchain with a fixed-price token that could only be used for consumption. Those facts are inapplicable to most crypto projects.

In August 2019, the SEC issued its second (and most recent as of this writing) No Action Letter to Pocketful of Quarters (PoQ). PoQ's tokens, called Quarters, are designed to serve as a universal currency in video games. According to PoQ, Quarters will allow gamers whom have earned rewards in one game to convert those in-game rewards to Quarters, and use those Quarters in other games and platforms.

As a condition to granting the PoQ No Action letter, the company had to assure the SEC that gamers would not be allowed to buy, sell, or exchange Quarters with other players, and developers and influencers would have to pass AML/KYC checks before they could open PoQ accounts. Like the TKJ token, Quarters would be issued on a permissioned, centralized blockchain with a fixed-price token used only for consumption. The PoQ No Action Letter broke little-if-any new ground.

Exemptions from Registration

Companies looking to offer or sell securities (issuers) must generally either register the offering with the SEC or seek an exemption from registration. In order to register, issuers must fully disclose any and all material information that a reasonable investor would require in making an investment decision.

To make compliance easier for smaller and newly public companies seeking to issue securities, the SEC offers a limited number of registration exemptions for:

- private offerings to a limited number of persons or institutions;
- offerings of limited size;
- intrastate offerings; and
- securities of municipal, state, and federal governments.

All securities transactions, whether exempt or not, are subject to the antifraud provisions of the federal securities laws. Both federal law, as well as state securities laws (called "Blue Sky laws"), provide for both civil and criminal penalties for fraud.

For companies seeking to raise money through issuances of securities, the process got easier beginning in 2012, when the Obama Administration and Congress enacted the Jumpstart Our Business Startups (JOBS) Act. The JOBS Act and its implementing regulations, coupled with existing laws, made it easier for companies to raise money within the parameters of US securities laws. Although the JOBS Act was passed in 2012, it took the SEC almost four years to finalize regulations explaining its provisions.

The JOBS Act, coupled with existing law, provided three attractive avenues for crypto companies seeking registration exemptions: Regulation A+ (Reg A+), Regulation CF (Reg CF) and Rule 506(c) of Regulation D (Reg D). Rules 504 and 506(b) of Reg D also offer crypto companies more traditional registration exemption options. Before discussing each exemption, a few key terms are defined below:

Key Terms

Accredited Investor

An "accredited investor" includes a natural person who:

- earned income that exceeded $200,000 (or $300,000 together with a spouse) in each of the prior two years, and reasonably expects the same for the current year; or

- has a net worth over $1 million, either alone or together with a spouse (excluding the value of the person's primary residence).

An "accredited investor" may also be an entity such as a bank, partnership, corporation, nonprofit or trust, when the entity satisfies certain criteria.

In December 2019, for the first time since 1983, the SEC proposed expanding the definition of accredited investor. Under the proposal, the definition would be expanded to include individuals holding certain securities licenses (Series 7, 65 or 92), private fund employees, registered investment advisers, family offices (and their clients) with $5 million under management, and limited liability companies, among others. The comment period for the

SEC proposal ended on April 24, 2020, and a final proposal is expected in the third quarter of 2020.

General Solicitation

"General solicitation" includes advertisements published in newspapers and magazines, public websites, communications broadcasted over television and radio, and seminars where attendees have been invited by general solicitation or general advertising. In addition, the use of an unrestricted, and therefore publicly available, website constitutes general solicitation.

Preemption

Some SEC exemptions "preempt" state securities laws, meaning the offering need not be registered with state regulators, nor follow state Blue Sky laws.

Restricted Securities

Securities that are not freely tradeable. In order to sell a restricted security to the public, five conditions must generally be met:

1. Holding Period: the security must typically be held for 6 to 12 months.

2. Current Public Information: information regarding the nature of the issuer's business, the identity of its officers and directors, and its financial statement must be publicly available.

3. Trading Volume Formula: any sales by parties affiliated with the issuer cannot exceed one percent of the outstanding shares of the same class as the securities being sold, or if listed on a stock exchange, the greater of one percent or the average

reported weekly trading volume during the four weeks preceding the filing of a notice of sale.

4. <u>Ordinary Brokerage Transactions</u>: any sales by parties affiliated with the issuer must be handled in all respects as routine trading transactions, and brokers may not receive more than a normal commission. Neither the seller nor the broker can solicit orders to buy the securities.

5. <u>Filing Requirement</u>: parties affiliated with the issuer must file a notice with the SEC if their proposed sale involves more than 5,000 shares or the aggregate dollar amount is greater than $50,000 in any three-month period.

The Exemptions

Reg A+

Through Reg A+ (sometimes called a mini-IPO), US or Canadian issuers can raise up to $50 million in a 12-month period from an unlimited number of non-accredited investors (the public) without registration as a public offering. Reg A+ offerings are subject to SEC review and qualification, and if approved, preempt state Blue Sky laws. Securities sold in a Reg A+ offering are not considered restricted securities.[40] However, securities purchased pursuant to a Reg A+ exemption cannot be listed or quoted on a securities exchange without registration.[41]

Reg A+ offerings have two tiers:

Tier 1: for offerings of up to $20 million in a 12-month period; and

---

[40] See Securities Act Rule 144.
[41] Registration would be under Section 12(b) of the Exchange Act.

Tier 2: for offerings of up to $50 million in a 12-month period.

For offerings of up to $20 million, companies can elect to proceed under the requirements for either Tier 1 or Tier 2.

As part of the Reg A+ approval process, a company can confidentially submit its offering memorandum to the SEC, allowing the company to gauge the SEC's reaction to the exemption. In addition, before committing to a Reg A+ offering, the SEC will allow a company to "test the waters" by polling its customers or the public about the investment before the company commits to spending considerable time and money on the SEC approval process.

Testing the waters allows a company to gauge the potential success of a Reg A+ offering in order to make an informed decision on whether to move forward. In general, during a "test the waters" campaign, a company invites potential investors (including customers) to indicate their interest in the company's securities. If there is not enough interest, the company can avoid the costs involved in proceeding with the offering.

In theory, the Reg A+ process should allow a company to enjoy a streamlined, expedited review process. In practice, however, the Reg A+ process has not been expedited for crypto-securities. Historically, companies seeking to offer securities under Reg A+ could expect approval within three months. However, despite the fact that early crypto-securities projects filed requests to offer securities under Reg A+ as early as mid-2017, no "true" crypto projects (see box below) were approved until the Blockstack Reg. A+ approval in July 2019.

The StartEngine Reg A+ Qualified Approval

One crypto-based company that was preliminarily approved to offer securities under Reg A+ was StartEngine, but the conditions of that approval are such that it is generally not regarded as a "true" crypto project. StartEngine, founded in 2014, claims to be the largest US equity crowdfunding platform, whose mission is to help entrepreneurs achieve their dreams by democratizing access to capital. In June 2018, StartEngine successfully raised nearly $5 million in a standard (i.e., non-crypto) Reg A+ offering.

After that first Reg A+ offering, StartEngine sought approval to issue tokenized equity securities under Reg A+. In its preliminary offering circular for the tokenized equity, StartEngine stated that it planned to issue common and preferred stock "in the form of electronic tokens". . . to "be delivered on the Ethereum Blockchain using a smart contract." However, after submitting its initial application, StartEngine was required to amend its preliminary offering circular six times before the SEC "qualified" its offering. A "qualified" offering means that the company may make sales of the securities described by the offering statement; it does not mean the SEC has approved, passed upon the merits or passed upon the accuracy or completeness of the information in the offering statement.

In that sixth version of its preliminary offering circular (dated March 7, 2019), almost all references to tokens and smart contracts were removed, as was the option of purchasing StartEngine's tokenized equity with crypto. In addition, StartEngine amended its charter to change the name of its securities from "Series Token Preferred Stock" to "Series T Preferred Stock." Effectively, StartEngine's approval was based on the SEC requiring them to remove from their offering nearly everything that was linked to crypto.

In April 2019, Blockstack, a New York-based blockchain software provider, announced that it had filed an offering statement with the SEC seeking to become the first "true" Reg A+ token offering.

According to Blockstack's website:

> *Blockstack Token LLC, our wholly-owned subsidiary, today announced that it has filed an offering statement with the Securities and Exchange Commission (SEC) to conduct a $50 million token offering using the SEC Regulation A+ framework. Upon approval, the offering is expected to be the first SEC-qualified token offering of its kind. The net proceeds of the offering will be used to accelerate the development of the Blockstack decentralized computing network and app ecosystem.*

Blockstack's received its Reg A+ approval in July 2019, and in September, raised over $23 million in the first SEC-qualified Reg A+ token offering. Although the Blockstack approval provided welcomed clarity regarding the SEC's Reg A+ requirements, it raised a host of other questions, including:

- *If the purchasers of Blockstack tokens spend the tokens in exchange for other goods or services, would the SEC consider that a sale of Blockstack securities?*

- *Can Blockstack token holders resell tokens to others?*

- *If an application accepts Blockstack tokens as payment, or uses the tokens to pay others, is the application soliciting the purchase of securities or acting as a securities dealer?*

- *Because the SEC approved the offering, is Blockstack exempt from New York's BitLicense regime?*

Another open question arising out of the Blockstack offering relate to mining. The Blockstack protocol relies on miners to mine "Stacks" tokens (STX). In the event that miners are issued over $50 million of STX tokens (the Reg A+ Tier 2 limit), it is unclear (i) how those tokens could be issued consistent with the securities laws, and (ii) whether the issuance of STX tokens to miners would be considered a separate offering.

Reg CF

Through Reg CF (officially "Regulation Crowdfunding," but commonly called Reg CF), issuers can raise up to $1 million (with adjustments for inflation) from non-accredited investors through SEC-approved broker-dealers or funding portals (see box below). Reg CF provides a simple and straightforward option for issuers, but, as of 2020, is limited to issuances of no more than $1.07 million.

What is a Funding Portal?

As part of the JOBS Act, the concept of an equity crowdfunding portal was created to allow entrepreneurs, startups, and nontraditional investment funds to raise funds from the public. To mitigate the fraud risks, Reg CF prohibits equity crowdfunding portals from:

- offering investment advice or recommendations to investors;

- soliciting purchases, sales, or offers to buy securities offered or displayed on their websites or portals;

- compensating employees, agents, or other persons for such solicitation or based on the sale

---

> of securities displayed or referenced on their websites or portals;
>
> - holding, managing, possessing, or otherwise handling investor funds or securities; or
>
> - engaging in activities the SEC, by rule, determines inappropriate.
>
> Equity crowdfunding portals share similarities with donation-based crowdfunding portals like Kickstarter. However, with equity crowdfunding, investors purchase shares in the company instead of a product or service.

Reg D

Through Reg D, issuers can raise potentially unlimited amounts of money from the sale of restricted securities. As part of a Reg D offering, issuers provide prospective investors with offering documents explaining the offering. Three rules-based Reg D offerings are Rule 504, Rule 506(b) and Rule 506(c). Each differs in the amount of money that can be raised, the acceptable investors, and the type of permissible solicitations. The provisions of each rule are outlined briefly below.

Rule 504

Rule 504, which does not preempt state law, allows an issuer to raise $5,000,000 of restricted securities in any 12-month period. Investors in offerings under Rule 504 should be informed that they may not be able to sell the securities for at least a year unless the issuer registers the resale transaction with the SEC. For the most part, general solicitation is prohibited in Rule 504 offerings, but there is a provision in Rule 504 that allows general solicitation based on state laws.

Rule 506(b) and (c)

Under Rules 506(b) and (c), which both preempt state law, an issuer can raise an unlimited amount of money from selling restricted securities. The differences are:

Under Rule 506(b), an issuer:

- can sell restricted securities to an unlimited number of accredited investors and up to 35 non-accredited investors;

- cannot use general solicitation or advertising to market the restricted securities; and

- must make itself available to answer questions by prospective purchasers.

In contrast, under Rule 506(c), an issuer:

- can only sell restricted securities to accredited investors; and

- can solicit and generally advertise the offering only to accredited investors.

Both Rules 506(b) and (c) require issuers to take reasonable steps to verify that the investors are accredited investors, which could include reviewing documentation, such as W-2s, credit reports, tax returns, as well as financial statements.

Exemptions from Registration	Reg A+		Reg CF	Reg D		
	Tier 1	Tier 2		Rule 506(b)	Rule 506(c)	Rule 504
Annual Offer Limit	$20M	$50M	$1.07M	None	None	$5M
General Solicitation	Permitted	Permitted	Permitted (limits on advertising)	No	Yes	Permitted with limits
Investor Requirements	None	Non-Accredited Investors subject to limits	Income and net worth limitations	Unlimited Accredited Investors	Unlimited Accredited Investors	None
SEC Requirements	• Form 1-A • Two years audited financial statements	• Form 1-A • Two years audited financial statements	• Form C • Two years audited financial statements	Form D	Form D	Form D
Resale Restrictions	No	No	12 months restriction	Restricted	Restricted	Restricted
State Preemption	No	Yes	Yes	Yes	Yes	Yes

A New Financial Product: A Bitcoin ETF

In addition to traditional securities like stocks, the SEC also regulates the offer and sale of pooled investment products available to the general public, including exchange-traded funds (ETFs). ETFs are investment funds comprised of baskets of different securities, indexes, commodities, bonds, or other assets. At the end of 2019, ETFs had a market capitalization of over $3 trillion, with the top ten ETFs holding assets valued at over $900 billion, and over 650 million ETF shares trading daily. The box below explains how ETFs work.

How ETFs Work

Shares in an ETF represent fractional interests in the pool of assets held by the ETF, and trade on exchanges like the New York

Stock Exchange or NASDAQ just like stocks. Each ETF share represents a fixed percentage of the ETF's net asset value (NAV), so as prices of the ETF's assets go up, so do the prices of ETF shares. One of the most popular ETFs is the iShares Core Standard & Poor's (S&P) 500 ETF (ticker symbol IVV), which tracks the investment results of an index composed of the S&P 500—the 500 public US companies with the largest market capitalization.

ETFs are structured as passive investment vehicles, in contrast to mutual funds that are actively managed by fund managers who pick the mutual fund's investments. Many brokers do not charge commissions for ETF purchases, nor do they impose minimum investment requirements. In contrast, mutual funds often require a minimum investment and charge brokerage fees for trades.

Because ETFs have no active managers, their expenses are typically small relative to mutual fund expenses. For example, the iShares Core S&P 500 ETF, as of April 2020, showed an expense ratio of 0.04 percent, while the average mutual fund had an expense ratio of between 0.5 and 1.0 percent, with some as high as 1.4 percent. In addition to having lower expenses, ETFs often outperform mutual funds. For example, *Barron's* reported that only three of the top 20 actively-managed equity mutual funds outperformed the S&P 500 index as of November 2019, and of those three, only one was open to new investors.[42]

The number of ETF shares is regulated through a mechanism known as creation and redemption, a function of the market demand for the underlying assets. That creation and redemption mechanism relies on entities known as "authorized participants"

---

[42] Andrew Barry, *Only 3 of the Top 20 Mutual Funds Are Beating the Market. Here's How They Do It.*, Barron's (Nov. 15, 2019).

who are contractually responsible for acquiring and disposing of assets on behalf of the ETFs. The mechanism operates as follows:

> Creation: When an ETF wants to create new ETF shares, the ETF directs the authorized participants to first buy more of the underlying assets, and then sell those assets to the ETF for new ETF shares. The authorized participants then sell the new ETF shares on the open market.

> Redemption: When an ETF wants to reduce the number of ETF shares, the ETF directs the authorized participants to first buy ETF shares on the open market, and then sell those shares back to the ETF in exchange for the underlying ETF assets. The authorized participants then sell those assets on the open market.

The SEC has not approved any Bitcoin ETF proposals, despite receiving proposals from as far back as 2016. A Bitcoin ETF is expected to increase demand for bitcoin because the investing public will be able to indirectly purchase bitcoin through traditional securities brokers and exchanges, without the need for a crypto wallet, a private key, or any of the technology-related things that have tended to limit the appeal of crypto to the broader investing public.

Approval of a Bitcoin ETF is also expected to generate more investment from institutional investors. To date, many of those investors have shied away from direct investments in crypto, often because of the custody risk of holding private keys, or because regulations or their operating rules prevent them from investing in non-regulated financial products.

Once a Bitcoin ETF is approved, demand from institutional investors is likely to increase. One reason for that is because the market performance of bitcoin has generally been uncorrelated to the performance of the stock market, as well as most other financial assets. As a result, according to modern portfolio theory,[43] holding bitcoin will help portfolios maximize expected returns for a given level of risk.

Whether a Bitcoin ETF *will* increase demand for bitcoin, and thereby the price of bitcoin, is anyone's guess. However, the history of the first gold ETF does lend support to the idea that a Bitcoin ETF would increase the BTC price. When the first gold ETF came to market in 2003, gold experienced a steady increase in price over the next ten years or so. However, whether, and the extent to which, the gold ETF *caused* the price increase is debatable, to say the least. As the saying goes, correlation does not equal causation.

What's the holdup?

The SEC has stated that it will approve a Bitcoin ETF once it determines that such an ETF is safe for the investing public. The articulated reasons the SEC has rejected Bitcoin ETF proposals include:

- the bitcoin market is easily manipulated;
- there are inadequate custody solutions available for securely holding bitcoin;
- there is no uniform price for bitcoin, with different exchanges quoting different prices; and
- the market for bitcoin is illiquid.

History of Bitcoin ETF proposals

The first Bitcoin ETF proposal was submitted by the Bats BZX exchange and the Winklevoss twins (the early Facebook investors)

---

[43] Modern portfolio theory is an investment theory that posits investors assemble asset portfolios that minimize idiosyncratic risk by holding diversified, uncorrelated assets. According to the theory, such portfolios maximize expected returns for a given level of risk.

in June 2016. The SEC ultimately rejected their proposal in March 2017, claiming the market for bitcoin was easily manipulated, volatile, and resistant to surveillance. Two weeks after the BZX/Winklevoss proposal was rejected, the SEC rejected another proposal, this time from NYSE Arca, a subsidiary of the New York Stock Exchange.

In 2018, the SEC rejected a revised BZX/Winklevoss proposal, but SEC commissioner Hester Peirce publicly dissented from the decision, writing:

> *"The disapproval order focuses on the characteristics of the spot market for bitcoin, rather than on the ability of BZX—pursuant to its own rules—to surveil trading of and to deter manipulation in the . . . shares listed and traded on BZX."*[44]

At the time, many thought Peirce's public comments were indicative of changing attitudes at the SEC. However, nine were rejected on August 22, 2018 alone, and no proposals have been approved as of this writing.

Although no proposals have been approved, two glimmers of hope came in February 2019, when:

- SEC commissioner Robert J. Jackson Jr, publicly pondered:

  > *"Eventually, do I think someone will satisfy the standards we've laid out there? I hope so, yes, and I think so,"*[45]

  and later added:

---

[44] See Dissent of Commissioner Hester M. Peirce to Release No. 34-83723; File No. SR-BatsBZX-2016-30, SEC Public Statement (Jul. 26, 2018).

[45] Chris Marquette, *Crypto-based funds crawl toward mom and pop*, Roll Call (Feb. 6, 2019).

> *"when the markets reach that stage, I fully believe we will have an SEC that's ready to approve a bitcoin ETF."*[46]

- Brian Quintenz, a Commodities and Futures Trading Commission (CFTC) commissioner criticized the SEC for having rejected previous ETFs on the grounds of potential price manipulation, stating:

> *"There are mathematical ways through a settlement index to design a contract where even if there isn't a lot of liquidity on one exchange referenced, the index itself is not readily susceptible to manipulation."*[47]

In a 112-page decision handed down in October 2019, the SEC rejected an amended Bitcoin ETF proposal filed in January 2019 from Bitwise and NYSE Arca. In the decision, the SEC noted that it remained concerned about market manipulation, and cited Bitwise's research suggesting only about 5 percent of the reported bitcoin trading volume was "real," and the other 95 percent was "fake." Bitwise's research indicated the fake trades included artificial trades between account holders on unregulated exchanges and wash trades (buy and sell orders often appearing in pairs, with one neutralizing the other) used to spike volume. In its decision, the SEC noted:

> *[Bitwise] has not established that it has in fact identified the "real" bitcoin market, or that the "real" bitcoin market is isolated from the fraudulent and manipulative activity.*

---

[46] Remarks of Robert Jackson, SEC Commissioner, 2019 Future of Fintech conference, CBInsights (Jun. 13, 2019).

[47] Remarks of Brian Quintenz, CFTC Commissioner, *The Year Ahead for Capital Markets*, Bipartisan Policy Center (Feb. 12, 2019).

Some legal analysts do not believe a Bitcoin ETF will be approved until the term of Jay Clayton, the current SEC Chair, ends. Clayton has long been a critic of the bitcoin market, and in September 2019 said:

> *"how can we be sure that those [bitcoin] prices [traded on unregulated exchanges] aren't subject to significant manipulation? . . . People need[ ] to answer these hard questions for us to be comfortable that [a Bitcoin ETF] was the appropriate kind of product."*[48]

ETF Trends CEO Tom Lydon has speculated that there is a 60 percent chance a Bitcoin ETF will be approved in 2020. Others, however, are less optimistic. CNBC analysist Bob Pisani neatly summed up the thoughts of the doubters:

> *The SEC is terrified grandma is going to buy a Bitcoin ETF that is going to collapse, and five years later, all the people running the SEC are going to get hauled in front of Congress and get [asked], 'Are you the guys who approved grandma buying the Bitcoin ETF?'"*[49]

---

[48] Remarks of Jay Clayton, SEC Chairman, 2019 Delivering Alpha conference hosted by CNBC and Institutional Investor (Sep. 19, 2019).

[49] Kyle Torpey, *Analyst: 60% Chance Of Bitcoin ETF In 2020*, Forbes (Jan. 14, 2020).

Commodities, Derivatives and the CFTC

The CFTC was created by the Commodities Exchange Act of 1936 (CEA) to regulate commodities, futures, options, and other derivatives markets. Its mission is to promote the integrity, resilience, and vibrancy of the US derivatives markets through sound regulation. In advancing that mission, the CFTC regulates key participants in the commodities and derivatives markets.

Although the CEA gives the CFTC exclusive jurisdiction only over derivative markets, the CFTC has historically had anti-fraud and anti-manipulation enforcement authority over certain spot markets (see box at right). That exercise of jurisdiction over spot markets is based, in part, on how fraud and manipulations in spot markets can generate profits in derivative markets.

> **Spot Markets**
>
> In a spot market, tangible assets like commodities and securities are traded for immediate delivery and payment. They are called spot markets because transactions are executed and settled "on the spot."

In a derivatives market, **_derivatives contracts_** (see box below) based on tangible or intangible assets are traded.

> **Derivatives Contract**
>
> A legal contract between two or more parties in which the value of the contract is based on the price of an agreed-upon underlying financial asset (like a security or a bushel of corn) or set of assets (like an index). Derivative contracts allow investors to use leverage (other people's property or money) in making investments.

For example, assume a stock was priced at $10 per share and Bibi believes the price will increase to $17 per share. If she wanted to make an investment in that stock, she could purchase 100 shares of that stock for $1,000 in a spot transaction. Alternatively, she could purchase a call option, a type of derivative that would give her the right, but not the obligation, to purchase 100 shares of the stock for $10 per share at some time in the future, regardless of the future price. For this example, assume the price of the call option is $150.

If Bibi were correct and the price increased from $10 to $17, the gain from the stock position would be $700, equal to the 100 shares × the $7 increase in price. At that point:

- if Bibi purchased the stock, her return on investment would be 70 percent, based on her $700 gain and her $1,000 investment;

- if she purchased the call option, she could (1) exercise that option and buy 100 shares at the $10 contract price (-$1,000), then (2) immediately sell those 100 shares for the current $17 price (+$1,700). Her gain would be calculated as follows:

Cost of option	($150)
Cost to exercise option	($1,000)
Sale of shares	$1,700
Gain	$550

  As a result, her return on investment would be 550 percent—a $550 gain from a $100 investment.

Based on the above example, Bibi's 550 percent return on investment from the call option far exceeds the 70 percent return she would have earned by purchasing the stock. In a nutshell, that example explains the attraction of derivatives.

While derivatives allow investors to increase their return on investments if prices move in their direction, they also increase the riskiness of those investments. Using the example above, if the price of the stock remained constant:

- if Bibi purchased the stock, she would have no gain or loss, and would keep her 100 shares of stock;

- if she purchased the call option, she would lose her entire $150 investment, because the right to purchase something for $10 when it is worth $10 has no value.

A popular derivatives contract is a futures contract, which is a legal agreement to buy or sell a particular asset at a predetermined price sometime in the future. The buyer of a futures contract is taking on the obligation of buying the underlying asset at a specified price when the contract ends (expiration), and the seller of the contract is taking on the obligation of selling the underlying asset at that price to the buyer at expiration. A futures contract, unlike a call option, does not give the buyer the option of making the purchase of the underlying asset in the future: buyers of futures contracts obligate themselves to acquire the asset, regardless of the actual price at expiration.

In the US, the CFTC oversees the regulation of futures contracts, ensuring they are standardized for quality and quantity. The 1983 movie *Trading Places,* starring Eddie Murphy, Dan Ackroyd, and Jamie Lee Curtis, does a fairly good job (between jokes) demonstrating how futures markets operate, using frozen concentrated orange juice futures contracts.[50] The movie also demonstrates the potential for manipulation and profit from futures markets, and why it is important that such markets be regulated.

Unlike most regulators around the world, the CFTC does not approve new financial products. Instead, it allows licensed exchanges to self-certify new products, so long as the exchanges assure the products meet the CFTC's core guidelines and principles. As part of the self-certification process, the CFTC staff coordinates with the exchanges to ensure new products comply with the CEA and CFTC regulations. From 2000 to 2019, exchanges and other market participants have self-certified over 12,000 products through the CFTC.

Prior to 2015, it was unclear whether the CFTC would exercise jurisdiction over crypto. Clarity came in September 2015, when the CFTC instituted a proceeding against Coinflip, a platform that facilitated bitcoin derivative contracts. In its order of settlement with Coinflip, the CFTC stated that bitcoin was a cryptocurrency, but because cryptocurrencies are not legal tender, the CFTC would not treat them as currencies. Instead, the CFTC would treat them as commodities. Consequentially, as commodities, bitcoin derivative contracts were subject to CFTC regulation under the CEA.

As a condition to its settlement with the CFTC, Coinflip admitted that the bitcoin derivative contracts it offered on its platform violated the CEA. After the settlement, two federal courts confirmed the CFTC position that certain crypto were commodities under the CEA, thus subject to CFTC regulation.[51]

According to the CFTC, its regulatory approach to crypto involves:

---

[50] In the movie, the trading took place on the floor of a futures exchange. Today, most futures trading takes place online.

[51] See *CFTC v. Patrick McDonnell et al.*, 332 F. Supp. 3d 641 (E. D. NY Aug. 28, 2018), and *CFTC v. My Big Coin Pay, Inc.*, 334 F. Supp. 3d 492 (D. MA Sep. 26, 2018).

Consumer Education. Amidst the wild assertions, bold headlines, and shocking hyperbole, there is a need for greater public understanding.

Asserting Legal Authority. Asserting legal authority over virtual currency derivatives in support of the CFTC's anti-fraud and manipulation efforts, including in underlying spot markets, is a key component in the CFTC's ability to effectively regulate these markets.

Market Intelligence. Gaining the ability to monitor markets for virtual currency derivatives and underlying settlement reference rates through the gathering of trade and counterparty data will provide regulatory and enforcement insights into those markets.

Robust Enforcement. In addition to its general regulatory and enforcement jurisdiction over the virtual currency derivatives markets, the CFTC has jurisdiction to police fraud and manipulation in cash or spot markets. The CFTC intends to continue to exercise this jurisdiction to enforce the law and prosecute fraud, abuse, manipulation, or false solicitation in markets for virtual currency derivatives and underlying spot trading.

Government-Wide Coordination. The CFTC actively coordinates its approach to bitcoin and other virtual currencies with other Federal regulators, including the SEC, FBI, DOJ and the Financial Stability Oversight Council. The CFTC also coordinates with state entities, including state Attorneys General, in addition to working with the White House, Congress and other policy-makers.

In general, the CFTC takes a relatively hands-off approach to regulation. One reason for this is that exchanges regulated by the CFTC, including the Chicago Mercantile Exchange (CME) and the

CBOE Futures Exchange (CFE), have a long and successful history as self-regulatory organizations dealing with risky assets. Another reason has to do with the CFTC's former chair, Chris Giancarlo.

From June 2014 until July 2019, Giancarlo, known in the crypto community as "Crypto Dad," served as the 13th chairman of the CFTC. Giancarlo was appointed by President Obama and reappointed by the succeeding administration; his appointment was unanimously confirmed by the Senate each time.

Giancarlo has long been a proponent of creating a supportive regulatory environment for crypto. He has stated that his support for supportive crypto regulation is based on his observations of the evolution of internet regulation. In an address regarding crypto regulation, he stated:

> *Two decades ago, as the Internet was entering a phase of rapid growth and expansion, a Republican Congress and the Clinton administration established a set of foundational principles: the Internet was to progress through human social interaction, voluntary contractual relations and free markets. Governments and regulators were not to harm the Internet's continuing evolution. Because of this "do no harm" approach, the Internet created millions of jobs, transformed our economy forever and improved standards of living across the globe.*
>
> *Today, as you know, a new technology is at hand that may offer a similarly profound tool to share networks of information. Yet, its development is at risk of being stymied by disparate and uncertain regulation.*

—Special Address of CFTC Commissioner Giancarlo, Depository Trust & Clearing Corporation 2016 Blockchain Symposium (Mar. 29, 2016)

Since exercising jurisdiction over crypto in 2015, the CFTC has enforced laws prohibiting market manipulation of crypto-based derivatives, issued proposed guidance on defining spot and derivative markets for crypto, issued warnings about valuations and volatility in spot crypto markets, and addressed crypto Ponzi schemes. In addition to working to ensure crypto markets are financially sound, the CFTC has also exercised jurisdiction over crypto-based secured lending arrangements, as discussed later in this chapter.

A Hamstrung Regulator

While many would agree that the CFTC has done a commendable job regulating crypto, it lacks the legal authority to do more. Under current law, the CFTC:

> *"lacks the legal authority to partner and collaborate with outside entities engaging directly with FinTech and innovation within a research and testing environment, including when the CFTC receives something of value absent a formal procurement. The general rule is that without such authority, the CFTC must forego the increasing number of opportunities to engage in research that may benefit the derivatives markets that the agency oversees, as well as the CFTC's own activities."*

> —Remarks of CFTC Chairman Giancarlo, *The Digital Trinity: Technology, Markets, and Policy*, 4th Annual DC Blockchain Summit (Mar. 6, 2019)

Other international regulatory agencies have that authority. For example, in 2015, the UK's FCA created an innovation hub that allows both regulated and non-regulated FinTech firms to introduce innovative financial products to the market and test new ideas through its regulatory sandbox. If the Financial Services Innovation Act proposed by Rep. McHenry (discussed in the final chapter) is passed, the CFTC would be allowed to create such an innovation hub through the Act's permanent beta testing (regulatory sandbox) provisions.

CFTC Enforcement Activities

In 2019, the CFTC collected over $1.3 billion in regulatory penalties, a 40 percent increase from 2018. Roughly 65 percent of the CFTC's enforcement actions were brought against individuals and entities engaging in fraudulent schemes in connection with commodities and other derivatives. Increasingly, more and more of those enforcement actions involve crypto.

In 2019 alone, the CFTC undertook the following crypto-related enforcement actions:

- In October 23, in a case brought by the CFTC, a federal judge ordered two individuals and four corporate entities to pay $4.25 million in damages for fraud in connection with a binary options scam involving a worthless crypto called ATM Coin.

- On September 30, the CFTC charged a Nevada individual and corporation with fraud relating to an $11 million binary options scheme. According to the complaint, the defendants (i) solicited and accepted at least $11 million worth of bitcoin and US dollars to trade derivatives, and (ii) made false claims about their trading expertise and guaranteed returns of up to 300 percent. Rather than using the funds to trade as promised, the defendants misappropriated funds by (i) retaining participants' funds in the defendant's personal crypto wallets and (ii) using funds to pay off earlier investors (a Ponzi scheme).

The defendants then lied to participants in order to conceal their misappropriation.

- Also on September 30, the CFTC charged one individual, Jon Barry Thompson, with fraud, alleging he convinced clients to send approximately $7 million to fund phony bitcoin purchases.

- On June 18, the CFTC announced that it had charged UK-based crypto company Control-Finance Limited and its CEO with misappropriating 22,858.822 bitcoins (valued at the time at $147 million) from more than 1,000 victims.

Although garden-variety fraud makes up most of the CFTC's enforcement activity, it has also exercised its jurisdiction over activities that, although not fraudulent, fall within its regulatory purview. Two such activities are unregulated trading and secured lending.

<u>Unregulated Trading</u>

Under US law, a derivatives exchange or trading platform must register with the CFTC if they either solicit or accept orders from US customers. Since 2015, after it determined that certain crypto were commodities, the CFTC has maintained that crypto derivatives exchanges must be registered if they allow US persons to trade.

On March 11, 2019, 1pool Ltd., a Marshall Islands online trading platform, and its CEO agreed to pay almost $1 million to settle CFTC charges. As part of that settlement, 1pool admitted that it had (i) offered to US customers contracts that used bitcoin as collateral, (ii) failed to register with the CFTC, and (iii) failed to implement an adequate AML/KYC program.

Reports in late 2019 suggested the CFTC was investigating Hong Kong-based BitMEX, one of the world's largest trading platforms, for allowing US persons to trade on their platform. The case is seen by many in the industry as important because it has the potential to extend the reach of US regulation outside US borders.

BitMEX has rules and policies in place to prohibit US persons from using its platform and removes any US persons whom it discovers have flouted those rules. In fact, on the main bitmex.com website, users are greeted with the following message:

> **Attention—Important Notice**
>
> It is prohibited to access or use our services (including the BitMEX trading platform) if you are located, incorporated or otherwise established in, or a citizen or resident of, any "Restricted Jurisdiction" [which includes the US] under (and as that term is defined in) our *Terms of Service.*
>
> BitMEX reserves the right to immediately close the accounts and to liquidate the open positions of persons determined to have breached our Terms of Service.

However, as noted by BitMEX CEO Arthur Hayes, "it is possible clients mask[ ] their location by using virtual private networks to assign their computer an internet protocol address from a BitMEX-permitted country, tricking [the] filters [BitMEX] put in place."

One reason US investors attempt to trade on BitMEX in spite of the prohibition is that BitMEX offers financial products that are generally unavailable to US customers. One such financial product is XBTUSD BTC/USD contract, which offers leverage up to 100X. Using the XBTUSD contract, an investor could post 1 BTC and be allowed to buy 100 BTC using leverage (other people's property). In general, the XBTUSD contract would work as follows:

- If the BTC price appreciates, the payoff is 100-to-1.

- However, if the price of BTC depreciates by 1 percent, because of the 100-to-1 leverage, the investor would lose their entire 1 BTC investment.

If the CFTC were able to sustain an enforcement action against BitMEX despite BitMEX's efforts to block US users, any platform that has US users (regardless of the platform's efforts to prohibit US users) could likely also be subject to US enforcement actions. Moreover, simply being investigated by the CFTC has repercussions. For example, soon after it was reported that the CFTC was investigating, BitMEX saw a record outflow of about $530 million of funds, more than five times the amount it had experienced in any previous months. Nevertheless, at the end of 2019, BitMEX remained one of the top three crypto derivates exchanges, behind Korea's OKEx and Singapore-based Huobi.

Secured Lending

The other non-fraudulent crypto-related activity regulated by the CFTC is secured lending. Secured lending is the process of a borrower pledging some assets (for example, bitcoin) as collateral for a loan. Once the assets are pledged, they act as protection against financial loss for the lender. An example would be a secured loan for bitcoin in which a borrower posts $100, and a lender lends the borrower $900 so the borrower can purchase $1,000 of bitcoin. In that example, the lender would hold the $1000 of bitcoin until the borrower repaid the $900 borrowed plus interest. To hold the bitcoin collateral, the lender will generally hold the private keys to the bitcoin as security for the loan.

The issues surrounding secured lending of crypto first arose in 2016 in a proceeding against the crypto exchange Bitfinex. On its platform, Bitfinex allowed retail users to enter into loans secured by bitcoin. Bitfinex's role was to match lenders, who were willing to provide financing secured by bitcoin, with borrowers, who desired to make leveraged purchases of bitcoin. In addition, Bitfinex would monitor the lending agreement and hold the collateral. The CFTC determined that Bitfinex's secured lending services amounted to an offer of "financed retail commodity transactions," a transaction regulated by the CFTC under the CEA.

Prior to 2010, Bitfinex's secured lending of bitcoin would not have created any issues (ignoring for the moment the fact that there was no market for bitcoin in 2010). However, in 2010, the Dodd-Frank Wall Street Reform and Consumer Protection Act (Dodd-Frank) amended the CEA to change the way commodity-backed retail secured loans were regulated, bringing the Bitfinex secured lending service under the ambit of the CEA.[52] Without wading into the precise legal details, it would have been exceedingly difficult for Bitfinex to comply with the myriad CEA-based legal and regulatory requirements that would have allowed it to offer secured lending services to retail customers.[53]

Why is the CFTC involved in this?

If anyone wonders why the CFTC, which regulates commodities and derivatives, exercised jurisdiction over secured loans, it is for one simple reason: as an economic matter, a secured loan (like the one described above) operates almost exactly like a futures contract.

---

[52] Congress passed the changes to the CEA in 2010 in response to the *CFTC v. Zelener*, 373 F. 3d 861 (7th Cir. 2004). In that decision, the Seventh Circuit had to determine whether the CFTC could regulate contracts that were in form spot contracts, but in substance futures contracts. The court ruled that the form of the contracts would be respected, thus not subject to CFTC jurisdiction. To reverse the effects of the *Zelener* decision, Congress amended the CEA to give the CFTC jurisdiction over secured-lending type financing arrangements that operated like futures contracts.

[53] An exception to the CEA-based requirements does exist, and Bitfinex argued that the exception should apply to them. In very simplified terms, if a secured lending arrangement results in the "actual delivery" of the collateral within 28 days, it can be offered to retail customers. Bitfinex argued that because it recorded the borrower as the owner in its books, the borrower was the owner and Bitfinex had satisfied the "actually delivery" exception. The CFTC disagreed, finding that actual delivery would require Bitfinex to "actually deliver" the private keys to the borrower. Obviously, Bitfinex could not transfer the private keys, because if it did so, it would no longer have any control over the collateral, making the loan unsecured.

Both allow borrowers/investors to obtain price exposure to an asset by using leverage, and both allow borrowers/investors to profit from increases in the price of the asset.

Crypto Tax and the IRS

"Tax Rules Everything Around Me, TREAM"
—Ryan McNeil of Ernst & Young, paraphrasing Wu Tang Clan

The taxation of crypto is well-settled in some areas, but inconsistent or incoherent in others. One of the well-settled areas is that crypto will be treated as property for tax purposes. The IRS made that determination through Notice 2014-21 (Notice) and its accompanying frequently asked questions (FAQs, collectively with the Notice, the 2014 Guidance). The 2014 Guidance was welcomed, because prior to its issuance and despite numerous requests from taxpayers, the US Taxpayer Advocate,[54] as well as an array of business and professional groups, the IRS had issued no official guidance on the tax treatment of crypto.

Over five years later, in October 2019 the IRS issued its second crypto guidance, Revenue Ruling 2019-24 (Rev. Rul. 2019-24 or the Ruling) and accompanying FAQs (collectively, the 2019 Guidance). The IRS indicated that the 2019 Guidance was intended to expand upon the 2014 Guidance. Although 2019 Guidance answered many open questions regarding the tax treatment of crypto, it raised a host of others.

In December 2019, eight members of Congress wrote to IRS Commissioner Rettig (Congressional Letter) asking for clarification of the 2019 Guidance, noting:

> *Ambiguity [in the tax laws] impedes appropriate tax compliance and unfairly targets taxpayers who may not have the ability to understand the positions the IRS has*

---

[54] The Taxpayer Advocate, the organization inside the IRS whose job it is to advocate on behalf of taxpayers, had asked for such guidance as far back as 2008.

taken in these matters but who have taken a reasonable position (sic).[55]

On February 28, 2020, the American Institute of Certified Public Accountants (AICPA) also drafted a letter to the IRS (AICPA Letter) identifying specific areas warranting additional or updated guidance. Both the Congressional Letter and the AICPA Letter highlighted and addressed significant shortcomings of the 2019 Guidance.

The analysis of both the 2014 and 2019 Guidance is below.

2014 Guidance

The Notice answered one of the foundational questions regarding the tax treatment of crypto: how should taxpayers treat transactions involving crypto? The IRS answered by stating that crypto (called "virtual currencies"[56] by the IRS) would be treated as property under the US tax code (Code). That meant that *any* sale or exchange of crypto, no matter the size, would be a taxable transaction and would have to be reported on a tax return.

Under the Code, crypto could have arguably been treated as either currencies, commodities, securities, or property. By choosing to treat crypto as property, the Code requires that whenever a taxpayer exchanges crypto for any other property, the taxpayer must report any and gains or losses related to the exchange. Those gains or losses are generally calculated by subtracting the taxpayer's adjusted cost basis (see box) in the crypto exchanged from the fair market value (FMV) of any property received in the exchange.

---

[55] The letter is available at https://coincenter.org/files/2019-12/letter-to-irs-dec-20.pdf.

[56] The Notice defined a virtual currency as "a digital representation of value that functions as a medium of exchange, a unit of account, and/or a store of value," and added that virtual currencies could be "used to pay for goods and services, or held for investment."

That answer provided clarity, but was also unsatisfactory. Treating crypto as property meant that almost every crypto transaction, including using crypto to buy coffee at Starbucks, could be a taxable transaction which had to be reported on a tax return.

The Basics of Tax Basis

Tax basis is the cost associated with property for tax purposes, and is used to calculate gains or loss on the sale, exchange, or other disposition of property. For each individual purchase of crypto, calculating the tax basis is relatively simple: the cost of the crypto plus any acquisition costs. However, when it comes to sales or other exchanges, the situation gets a bit more complicated because it is often not apparent exactly which crypto is used in a sale or exchange.

For example, assume Bibi purchased one bitcoin every year on January 1, from 2011 to 2020, and now has 10 bitcoins. As noted in Part II, those bitcoins would have been purchased for anywhere between $0.30 per bitcoin (Jan. 2011 price) and $13,657 (Jan. 2018 price). Each of those 10 bitcoins would have its own tax basis, based on the purchase price of each. Now, if Bibi purchased a car from Chaun for 4.5 bitcoins on January 2, 2020, although the Notice directs Bibi to report the exchange of one property (4.5 bitcoins) for another (the car), it provided no guidance regarding how Bibi should determine *which* 4.5 of her 10 bitcoins were used to purchase the car.

While the Notice answered a foundational tax question, it failed to address numerous others, leaving taxpayers to their own devices to figure them out. In the five years after the 2014 Guidance was issued, both the American Bar Association (ABA) and the AICPA requested additional guidance from the IRS on a number of those open questions. One issue was the tax treatment of forks, which both the ABA and the AICPA noted that was one of the most pressing open questions facing taxpayers.

On May 16, 2019, IRS Commissioner Charles Rettig acknowledged the problems created by the IRS' failure to provide additional guidance, and sent a letter to Congress indicating that new crypto guidance was a priority, and it should be coming "soon." Commissioner Rettig's letter was in response to a request from 21 members of Congress who asked the IRS to provide clarity on tax reporting for crypto, noting that there was "substantial ambiguity on a number of important questions about the federal taxation" of crypto.

In Rettig's response, he stated, "I share your belief that taxpayers deserve clarity on basic issues related to the taxation of [crypto] transactions and have made it a priority of the IRS to issue guidance." Rettig added that one of the issues the IRS was working on was "acceptable methods for [determining] the tax treatment of forks." That guidance came in October 2019.

2019 Guidance

Rev. Rul. 2019-24 addressed the tax treatment of forks and airdrops. In doing so, it also addressed a sub-issue of both: when receiving a new crypto after a fork or airdrop, under what circumstances will a taxpayer be required to report income with respect to the new crypto. The FAQs issued along with Rev. Rul. 2019-24 provided guidance on a number of technical tax issues, including one of the most important for taxpayers: how they should calculate their tax basis in crypto.

Tax treatment of forks

Rev. Rul. 2019-24 defined a hard fork as occurring "when a [crypto] on a [blockchain][57] undergoes a protocol change resulting in a permanent diversion from the legacy or existing [blockchain]." In

---

[57]   The IRS used the term "distributed ledger."

the Ruling, the IRS made its position clear: if a taxpayer has "dominion and control" over a new coin after a fork, the taxpayer will have taxable income equal to the fair market value of the new coin when that new coin is recorded on the new blockchain. The IRS included the "dominion and control" language so that taxpayers would not be taxed in situations in which they hold crypto through an exchange or other intermediary that does not list or otherwise support the new crypto.[58] In such situations, the Ruling indicates that because such taxpayers have no ability to immediately spend or transfer those new unlisted/unsupported coins, they do not have to recognize income associated with those coins.

Tax treatment of airdrops

The Ruling defined an airdrop as "a means of distributing units of a [crypto] to the [blockchain] addresses of multiple taxpayers." The Ruling then added that crypto "from an airdrop generally is received on the date and at the time it is recorded on the [blockchain]." As was the case for hard forks, the IRS noted that "[a] taxpayer does not have receipt of [crypto] when the airdrop is recorded on the [blockchain] if the taxpayer is not able to exercise dominion and control over the [crypto]."

The Ruling noted that "a taxpayer may constructively receive [crypto] prior to the airdrop being recorded on the [blockchain]." However, the IRS provided no explanation or examples describing how a taxpayer could constructively receive crypto *before* it was recorded on a blockchain. Even if airdropped crypto were somehow constructively received before it was recorded on a blockchain, the Ruling provided no explanation regarding how a taxpayer could exercise "dominion and control" over such crypto.

---

[58] As noted in the Securities Law chapter, exchanges often do not list newly-issued coins. If a taxpayer wanted to receive the non-listed coins, the taxpayer would generally have to remove the coin from the exchange into either a private wallet or an exchange that listed the coin.

Basis of crypto

The FAQs accompanying the Ruling addressed the tax basis for crypto. Both the ABA and the AICPA had raised the issue, noting that without specific IRS guidance, taxpayers had to make educated guesses about how to calculate and track their crypto's basis. In other tax contexts, permissible methods to determine a property's basis include first-In, first-out (FIFO), last-in, last-out (LIFO), specific identification of the property used in a transaction, and the average-cost method.

The AICPA suggested the IRS should allow FIFO unless a taxpayer was able to identify the specific units of crypto used in a transaction. The IRS appears to have adopted the AICPA's suggestion. In FAQ 40, the IRS announced that unless a taxpayer identifies the specific units of crypto used in a transaction, the units are deemed to have been sold, exchanged, or otherwise disposed of in chronological order beginning with the earliest unit of the crypto purchased or acquired (i.e., FIFO).

Analysis of the 2019 Guidance

Although the 2019 Guidance provided answers to many open questions, it raised many other issues, including:

1) it failed to address a *de minimis* exception for small transactions;

2) it is unclear, imprecise, and in places inequitable; and

3) as guidance, it lacks the force of law or regulation, and is subject to challenge.

A *de minimis* exemption

The 2019 Guidance failed to address an exemption for smaller crypto transactions, despite many organizations, including both the

AICPA and the ABA, recommending such a provision. The IRS acknowledged the issue in a 2018 IRS Presentation, noting the AICPA's suggestion of creating an exemption for transactions below $200, similar to the *de minimis* exemption for personal foreign currency transactions.[59] Without such an exemption, taxpayers are required to report to the IRS *every* transaction in which crypto is used, from using bitcoin to purchase coffee at Starbucks to exchanging $1 of BTC for $1 of ETH. In the Feb. 2020 AICPA Letter, the AICPA asked the IRS to "exercise its administrative discretion to enforce the tax laws to create a *de minimis* safe harbor" to spare taxpayers the trouble of accounting for transactions "where the administrative costs outweigh any possible tax on the immaterial transactions."

The IRS has offered no explanation for not including a *de minimis* exception, but two possible rationales are:

1. IRS personnel believe such a rule would frustrate the IRS's attempts to have taxpayers report their crypto transactions. Many have speculated that a *de minimis* rule could lead to advanced tax avoidance techniques, such as structuring numerous transactions below the threshold (not really an advanced technique, but a good starting point for creating one). In addition, monitoring a *de minimis* rule would likely be more time intensive for the IRS, because it would not only require the IRS to examine all transactions, but also (i) first filter out transactions below the $200 threshold, and then (ii)

---

[59] The Presentation notes that it would be possible to structure such *a de minimis* election in a similar manner to the election under Section 988(e)(2) of the Code, passed by Congress in 1997. That section exempts taxpayers from reporting foreign currency gains for personal transactions up to $200, and a motivating factor for its passage was to exempt taxpayers who purchased foreign currency for vacation purposes from having to report gains related to changes in currency prices.

determine if a series of those filtered transactions were structured to avoid reporting.[60]

2. The IRS cannot create new law. It was Congress, not the IRS, who created the *de minimis* exemption for personal foreign currency transactions. Thus, absent a congressional directive to exempt crypto, the IRS cannot create a new law simply because it would be convenient for taxpayers.

In January 2020, a bill was introduced in Congress to address the *de minimis* exemption. The bill, entitled the Virtual Currency Tax Fairness Act of 2020,[61] was introduced with bipartisan support in the U.S. House Representatives. The bill excludes from gross income up to $200 of gain from the disposition of virtual currency in a personal transaction. A previous version of the bill, introduced in 2017, sought to exempt transactions in amounts below $600. In addition, both the 2018 and 2019 Token Taxonomy Acts (neither of which passed) included a $600 *de minimis* exemption.

<u>Poor Guidance</u>

The Dec. 2019 Congressional Letter notes that

> *"this recent guidance creates many new questions related to the topics it seeks to address, namely forks and airdrops. Moreover, [it] appears inequitable."*

Those questions make it difficult to determine how certain transactions should be treated. In the 2019 Guidance, the IRS defines a hard fork using the following language:

> *"a hard fork occurs when a [crypto] . . . undergoes a protocol change resulting in a permanent diversion from the legacy [blockchain], resulting in the creation of a new*

---

[60] As a former DOJ tax prosecutor, I can attest that such a concern is not without merit.

[61] H.R.5635

[crypto] on a new [blockchain] in addition to the legacy [crypto] on the legacy [blockchain]."

Later, the IRS uses the following language to define an airdrop:

"An airdrop is a means of distributing units of a [crypto] to the [blockchain] addresses of multiple taxpayers. A hard fork followed by an airdrop results in the distribution of units of the new [crypto] to addresses containing the legacy [crypto]."

Both definitions are imprecise. The hard forks related to Bitcoin Cash (BCH) and Ethereum Classic (ETC) demonstrate the imprecision, as described below.

Bitcoin Cash Hard Forks

On August 1, 2017, Bitcoin Cash (BCH) forked away from the Bitcoin (BTC) blockchain (the BTC/BCH fork), a fork that arguably fits the Guidance's definition, with BCH being the "new" crypto. However, contrary to the IRS definitions, the BCH was not "airdropped" to the existing BTC hodlers. Airdrops typically are newly-launched crypto that are assigned automatically to existing holders of tokens or coins on a network. In contrast, after a hard fork, particularly a contentious one, owners of the pre-forked coin (BTC) own, by right, both the new coin (BCH) and the existing coin (BTC).

After the BTC/BCH fork in 2017, BCH itself forked the following year into two coins, Bitcoin Cash Adjustable Blocksize Cap (ABC) and Bitcoin Satoshi's Vision (SV) (the ABC/SV fork). The 2019 Guidance creates confusion regarding how the ABC/SV fork would be treated for tax purposes, because after that fork, both coins made legitimate claims to be "legacy" coin, and both also claimed the other coin was the "new" coin.

Immediately after the ABC/SV fork, it was unclear which blockchain was the dominant one, and which would be able to call itself the "true" Bitcoin Cash (BCH). Some exchanges even halted trading for days on both ABC and SV until it was clear who the "winner" would be. Eventually, most exchanges recognized ABC as the winner, and allowed ABC to use the name Bitcoin Cash, and the ticker BCH.

Despite the uncertainty regarding which was the "new" coin and which was the "legacy" coin, the 2019 Guidance required taxpayers to report the FMV of the "new" coin as a gain. It is unclear how taxpayers are supposed to determine which is the new coin in such circumstances.

Ethereum Hard Fork

Another problem with the 2019 Guidance is highlighted by the July 2016 Ethereum/Ethereum Classic fork (the ETH/ETC fork) after The DAO hack. Soon after the hack, the Ethereum community decided to fork the Ethereum blockchain to undo the effects of the hack. To implement the fork, the Ethereum developers identified a pre-hack block of the Ethereum blockchain and forked the blockchain from that block.

The ETH/ETC fork had the effect of reversing most of the hack's effects on the Ethereum blockchain, and restoring much of the ETH misappropriated by the hacker to the original owners. However, some in the Ethereum community rejected the hard fork, essentially arguing that an "immutable" blockchain should not have an "undo" feature. Their response was to ignore the ETH fork, and they began mining blocks on the original, non-forked version of Ethereum, creating Ethereum Classic (ETC).

From a technical perspective, ETC would appear to be the legacy chain. It represents the "unforked" original Ethereum chain. At the time of the ETH/ETC fork, ETH was over 1,500 percent more valuable than ETC. During that time, ETC opened trading in July 2016 at around $0.75, while ETH was trading between $11.50 – $14.44, and did not change appreciably in the days following the fork. If the 2019 Guidance (which is retroactive) is followed, taxpayers would be required to report the entire value of their ETH holdings as a gain at the July 2016 price, and any basis they had in the pre-forked ETH would go to ETC. That nonsensical result is arguably required under the 2019 Guidance.

Does it matter which is the "new" coin?

Yes. Ambiguities in tax laws makes it more difficult for taxpayers to accurately report their income. In addition, a significant portion of taxpayer non-compliance is attributed to tax code complexity and ambiguity.[62]

What is the FMV of the "new" coin?

Q&A 23 in the 2019 Guidance's FAQs states that:

> *you will have ordinary income equal to the fair market value of the new [crypto] when it is received, which is when the transaction is recorded on the [blockchain], provided you have dominion and control over the [crypto] so that you can transfer, sell, exchange, or otherwise dispose of the [crypto].*

---

[62] See generally, *Complexity in the Federal Tax System*, Joint Committee on Taxation (Mar. 6, 2015).

That language does not provide clear guidance on exactly when a taxpayer will have income. As a preliminary matter, as noted in the AICPA Letter:

> *"chain split coins have a zero or near-zero realizable value at the time of a split. . . [and] even if a chain split coin was considered to have a non-zero value at the time of a chain split, taxpayers often cannot claim the coins at that time because those coins are not supported by wallets or coin splitting services. While, in theory, taxpayers can exercise dominion and control by selling a paper wallet entitling the buyer to the chain split coins, in reality, taxpayers would not actually transact in that matter because that type of market would be illiquid, unregulated, and inefficient."*

The aftermath of the ABC/SV fork shows other problems with the IRS approach. On the day before the fork (Nov. 14, 2018), BCH closed at a price of $439.31. After that fork, the price of the new coins, ABC and SV, fluctuated wildly. The charts below show the prices, in dollar terms, of both ABC and SV during and after the fork:

ABC Chart

Dates	ABC Trading Prices			
	Open	High	Low	Close
November 15: Day of the fork	$439.96	$453.62	$403.75	$421.32
November 16: Day after the fork	$421.20	$423.43	$388.82	$388.82
December 8: A few weeks after the fork	$106.24	$109.96	$99.84	$104.05

SV Chart

Dates	SV Trading Prices			
	Open	High	Low	Close
November 15: Day of the fork	$176.28	$179.51	$70.97	$93.70
November 16: Day after the fork	$94.47	$134.29	$76.79	$122.97
December 8: A few weeks after the fork	$103.79	$104.08	$96.35	$98.68

Based on the above charts, it is unclear how taxpayers are to determine the FMV of the "new" coin when it is "received" and "recorded" on the blockchain. Of the array of prices in those charts, the IRS offers taxpayers no guidance on how they should determine which price to use, how they are to determine which is the "new" coin and when it was received, and when their ownership was recorded on the blockchain.

The ABC and SV charts also highlight a more practical problem: many taxpayers will be required to report income in situations in which they have losses. For example, the value of BCH prior to the fork, using the November 14 closing price, was $439.31. By December 8, the combined values of ABC and SV were $202.73, a loss of over $230. However, despite the economic loss, taxpayers would be required to report ordinary income in the amount of the FMV of the "new" coin. Forcing taxpayers to pay taxes at ordinary rates for phantom gains when they experience economic losses is bad public policy.

Other problems highlighted by the AICPA Letter are more practical. The IRS approach would be burdensome both to taxpayers and the IRS, and would require:

> "the IRS to administer, and taxpayers to apply, a realization rule that requires a case-by-case basis to determine the time at which a particular taxpayer can,

or should, exercise dominion and control over unsolicited, and possibly unwanted, property."

Moreover, trying to determine the values of that property:

"would create an undue burden for taxpayers and result in an unlimited number of approaches, inconsistently applied, [giving taxpayers] a range of reasonable approaches to determine the fair [market] value for chain splits, [and] airdrops."

In other countries, the taxation of hard forks is handled differently. In the UK for example, crypto received from a hard fork is not immediately subject to income tax. Instead, no taxes are due until the crypto has been sold or exchanged.

To calculate the cost basis of forked coins in the UK, taxpayers are instructed to apportion the tax basis between the old coins and the new coins, in a "just and reasonable" manner.[63] UK law does not prescribe any particular apportionment method; however, the standard practice in the UK is that the basis of the old crypto is apportioned between the old and new crypto assets in line with the market values of both on the day after the hard fork. If the IRS adopted the UK approach, many of the problems associated with the IRS-prescribed methods would disappear.

The 2019 Guidance concept of receipt of airdrops is also problematic. According the Guidance:

"Cryptocurrency from an airdrop generally is received on the date and at the time it is recorded on the distributed ledger. However, a taxpayer may constructively receive cryptocurrency prior to the airdrop being recorded on the distributed ledger. A taxpayer does not have receipt of cryptocurrency when the airdrop is recorded on the

---

[63]   See Section 52(4) Taxation of Capital Gains Act 1992 (UK).

distributed ledger if the taxpayer is not able to exercise dominion and control over the cryptocurrency."

Based on that concept of receipt, the ability to "exercise dominion and control over the crypto," makes the airdrop taxable, whether or not the taxpayer is aware of that ability.[64]

The Congressional Letter addressed this issue, (i) noting that the 2019 Guidance "appears to diverge from established rules in other areas," and (ii) suggesting airdrops be treated like the receipt of unsolicited property. The Feb. 2020 AICPA Letter also addressed the issue, noting the "IRS's long-standing policy—actual manifestation of acceptance of unsolicited property—has addressed the tax issues regarding unwanted property for many decades."

If airdrops were treated as unsolicited property, they would not be taxable unless and until a taxpayer manifests acceptance of the property by actually exercising dominion and control over it. Such treatment is consistent with existing law, as noted by the AICPA Letter:

> *The IRS and courts have, for many years, determined that unsolicited property is includible as income under section 61 only when the taxpayer manifests acceptance of the property by exercising dominion and control over it. This treatment is appropriate for purposes of determining the tax consequences of chain splits and airdrops for most taxpayers.*

Since 2014, there have been at least 74 passive BTC forks and airdrops, meaning projects have issued coins to existing BTC holders without any participation from those individuals. Because those existing BTC holders were "able to" exercise dominion and control over those airdropped coins, according to the 2019 Guidance, those

---

[64] The Guidance acknowledges that taxpayers who hold their crypto in exchanges that do not support the newly-created airdropped coins do not have dominion and control.

taxpayers were required to report the FMV of the airdropped coins as ordinary income, whether or not the taxpayers knew about the airdrops. Also problematic is the fact that many of those projects failed, resulting in worthless coins. As a result, taxpayers are faced with a tax on property they did not ask for, never used, and which later may become worthless.

To make matters worse for taxpayers, Revenue Ruling 2019-24 applies retroactively, and provides no safe harbors or transition relief. As a result, to comply with the 2019 Guidance, taxpayers may need to file amended returns at least three years back (six in certain circumstances).[65] For holders of BTC, that means they would have to file returns that included any of those 74 airdrops that were not worthless when dropped, whether or not those airdropped coins later became worthless.

The AICPA Letter also addressed the retroactivity of the Revenue Ruling, noting that, "Treasury and the IRS should issue proposed regulations before publishing guidance that is retroactively effective." The AICPA recommended providing a safe harbor for taxpayers, giving them transition relief for tax years prior to the 2019 Guidance.

The Weakness of Tax Guidance

One core problem with the 2019 Guidance is that it does not carry the force of law or regulation, meaning many of the issues it addresses may ultimately be decided by either the courts or Congress. Moreover, as noted in the AICPA Letter, guidance through FAQs is unreliable and "can change at any time and without notice." In addition, unlike FinCEN and SEC guidance, IRS guidance is easier and far less costly to challenge.

---

[65]   In general, the statute of limitations for tax returns is three years from the filing date, six years if the tax understatement is substantial, i.e., more than 25 percent of gross income. If a taxpayer failed to file a return, or filed a fraudulent return, the statute of limitations remains open.

Although revenue rulings like Rev. Rul. 2019-24 are official IRS interpretations of the Code, courts are not bound to follow them. Traditionally, courts apply what is known as *Skidmore* deference to revenue rulings, meaning that courts will look to the persuasiveness of a revenue ruling in making a decision. In contrast, tax regulations are afforded *Chevron* deference,[66] meaning, in general, courts will follow an IRS position regardless of whether the court might believe another position is better, so long as the IRS position is reasonable.

If a taxpayer disagrees with IRS guidance, the taxpayer can report a transaction inconsistent with the IRS guidance and wait to see whether the IRS will challenge the taxpayer's method of reporting. That, in turn, puts the burden on the IRS to first identify the inconsistent treatment among the millions of returns it has to process, then determine whether it should challenge the taxpayer. If hundreds or thousands of taxpayers make inconsistent reports, the IRS faces the dilemma of how to defend its position for all such taxpayers, and often offers settlements for pennies on the dollar instead of litigating all such challenges.[67]

When the IRS challenges a taxpayer's reporting method, it must expend resources determining the facts and negotiating with each such taxpayer, an expensive proposition even for the IRS. Moreover, before paying the tax, each of those taxpayers can challenge any ultimate IRS determinations by petitioning the US Tax Court, who are not bound by IRS determinations. Alternatively, after paying the

---

[66] Before applying *Chevron* deference to an IRS interpretation of a tax regulation, a court must generally find that (i) the underlying tax statute is ambiguous, and (ii) the IRS regulation is a reasonable interpretation of the ambiguous statute.

[67] For example, Son of Boss was the largest tax shelter in US history, and estimates suggest it allowed taxpayers to understate their tax liabilities by over $6 billion. The IRS offered a settlement to Son of Boss participants, and according to former IRS Commissioner Mark Everson, the IRS collected around $3.2 billion from the settlement. See Treasury Inspector General for Tax Administration, *Despite the Success Achieved, the Son of Boss Settlement Had Little Impact on Investor Filing and Payment Compliance*, Ref. No. 2009-30-018 (Dec. 30, 2018).

tax, taxpayers can sue for refund in federal court, and those courts are also not bound by IRS determinations.

In either case, if a court sides with the IRS, the costs to the taxpayer are generally only the back taxes and the cost of the challenge. So long as the taxpayer's position is reasonable, it is unlikely penalties will be imposed. As a result, taxpayers often view taking risky tax positions as a gambit, with the worst outcome being discovery by the IRS and payment of the tax three-to-six years down the road. That, coupled with the relatively small chance of detection (the IRS audited about 0.59 percent of individual returns in 2018), means that many taxpayers will at least entertain the idea of taking that gambit.

Another weakness of IRS guidance is that the costs of challenging it pales in comparison to the costs involved in challenging the SEC or FinCEN. Both agencies have the power to levy fines or bring criminal charges against individuals and entities they believe violate their guidance. As a result, the costs of squaring off in court against the SEC or FinCEN will often dwarf the costs of challenging the IRS. For example, it has cost Kik over $5 million to defend itself against the SEC (as described in the Securities Law chapter), and required thousands of hours of lawyers' time analyzing myriad legal and factual issues. In contrast, most IRS challenges involve facts that have been stipulated by both sides and a request to the court to determine how the law should apply to those facts, a far less expensive proposition.

It makes little sense for the IRS to issue unclear guidance that will encourage taxpayers to challenge it, forcing the IRS to waste precious resources on a self-inflicted wound. Hopefully, the IRS will adopt the AICPA recommendation and "issue guidance in the form of proposed regulations and allow a period for public comment. This process is consistent with the March 2019 Treasury policy statement expressing Treasury's preference for notice and rulemaking."[68]

IRS Enforcement

While the IRS did not issue much in the way of guidance prior to 2019, it nonetheless worked to ensure that the tax laws were enforced with respect to crypto. For example, in November 2016, the IRS issued a "John Doe" summons to Coinbase, seeking information about Coinbase customers' crypto transactions.

What is an IRS John Doe Summons?

A "John Doe" summons is an order that does not seek information about an identifiable person, but instead identifies a particular activity, and seeks information about persons or entities engaged in that activity. John Doe summonses are often used when the IRS believes taxpayers are engaged in improper conduct and can identify the types of transactions involved, but cannot identify the individual taxpayers.

Under Section 7609(f) of the Code, in order to obtain a John Doe summons, the IRS must convince a federal judge that:

1) the summons relates to the investigation of an ascertainable group or class of persons;

2) there exists a reasonable basis for believing that such group or class of persons may have failed to comply with US tax laws; and

---

[68] That policy statement, "allows the public to participate before any final rule becomes effective and ensures that all views are adequately considered. It also enables the public to apprise the government of relevant information that the government may not possess or to alert the government to consequences that it may not foresee." See Dept. of the Treasury, *Policy Statement on the Tax Regulatory Process* (Mar. 5, 2019).

> 3)   the information sought by the summons is not readily available from any other source.

In the John Doe summons issued to Coinbase, the IRS asked for:

- complete user profiles, history of changes to user profiles from account inception, complete user preferences, complete user security settings and history (including confirmed devices and account activity), complete user payment methods and any other information related to the funding sources for the account/wallet/vault, regardless of date;

- all records of account/wallet/vault activity including transaction logs or other records identifying the date, amount and type of transaction (purchase/sale/exchange), the post-transaction balance, the names or other identifiers of counterparties to the transaction, requests or instructions to send or receive bitcoin; and

- where counterparties transact through their own Coinbase accounts/wallets/vaults, all available information identifying the users of such accounts and their contact information.

The IRS claimed that it needed that information because it had found evidence of non-compliance with US tax laws by Coinbase customers, but could not determine the identities of those customers without the information from Coinbase. After receiving the summons, Coinbase refused to comply, and issued the following statement:

"Although Coinbase's general practice is to cooperate with properly targeted law enforcement inquiries, we are extremely concerned with the indiscriminate breadth

of the government's request. Our customers' privacy rights are important to us and our legal team is in the process of examining the government's petition. In its current form, we will oppose the government's petition in court. We will continue to keep our customers informed on developments in this matter."

Coinbase eventually challenged the summons in federal court, arguing the request was overbroad.

In the ensuing litigation, the IRS defended the summons by focusing on the problem of underreporting, noting:

"There has been an explosion of billions of dollars of wealth in just a few years from bitcoin, a significant amount of which has no doubt accrued to United States taxpayers, with virtually no third-party reporting to the IRS of that increase in income,"

and that some users of cryptocurrency:

"have openly acknowledged they consider using bitcoin in order to avoid tax reporting requirements."

Ultimately, the court narrowed the scope of the summons and required Coinbase to produce only the taxpayer identification information (social security or tax identification number, birthdate, address) and account activity records of its crypto customers. The court also told the IRS that if it needed more detailed records on a specific taxpayer, the IRS could issue a summons directly to the taxpayer or to Coinbase with notice to the taxpayer.

The IRS also stepped up its enforcement efforts in 2019. In July, it sent out three compliance-related letters based, in part, on the responses it received from the John Doe summonses. Those letters served as a warning to taxpayers to report their crypto transactions, with three levels of intensity. Some of the relevant language of each letter is included below:

<u>Letter 6174:</u>

"We have information that you have or had one or more accounts containing virtual currency but may not know the requirements for reporting transactions involving virtual currency."

<u>Letter 6174-A:</u>

"We have information that you have or had one or more accounts containing virtual currency but may not have properly reported your transactions involving virtual currency."

<u>Letter 6173:</u>

"We have information that you have or had one or more accounts containing virtual currency and may not have met your US tax filing and reporting requirements for transactions involving virtual currency." The Letter 6173 also required taxpayers to file a response either amending a return or providing documentation supporting the reporting position they took on their return.

<u>A Privacy Issue</u>

The IRS efforts at gathering information have not been limited to requests from third-parties. In the Schedule 1 for the 2019 tax year (the Schedule 1 is often filed along with the standard tax returns using the Form 1040), the IRS has included the following question (the crypto question):

"*At any time during 2019, did you receive, sell, send, exchange, or otherwise acquire any financial interest in any virtual currency?*"

Because the Form 1040 requires taxpayers to declare, under penalty of perjury, that the return and accompanying schedules are, to the best of a taxpayer's knowledge, "true, correct, and complete," the crypto question is tantamount to an IRS requirement that taxpayers disclose to the government whether they acquired crypto in 2019, regardless of whether they owe any crypto-related tax. In addition, responding inaccurately, or failing to answer the crypto question, could be considered filing a false tax return, a crime under 26 U.S.C. § 7206(1).

The AICPA Letter asked the IRS to provide needed clarity on some of the issues raised by the crypto questions, including:

1. *If an individual moves virtual currency from one wallet to another and has no other transactions with virtual currency, what answer should they select (is this situation considered an exchange)?*

2. *How should taxpayers report a virtual currency gift?*

3. *How can taxpayers disclose transactions if they own an interest in a partnership but do not know if the partnership received, sold, sent, exchanged, or otherwise acquired any virtual currency? Or is the question specific to the individual Form 1040 taxpayer's ownership (without considering any pass-through entity activity)?*

4. *Should taxpayers who claim a child or dependent credit for someone involved in or possibly involved in gaming answer "yes"?*

5. *When might certain gift cards or company online accounts constitute virtual currency for purposes of the new question?*

6. *What does the term "financial interest" mean?*

7.   *Should an individual who holds a virtual currency
        but who did not use it during the year answer "yes"?*

A question analogous to the crypto question on tax returns is the requirement that taxpayers disclose ownership or control over foreign bank accounts. On the Schedule B that accompanies the Form 1040, question 7a asks:

> *At any time during 2019, did you have a financial interest
> in or signature authority over a financial account (such as
> a bank account, securities account, or brokerage account)
> located in a foreign country?*

That foreign account question, like the crypto question, does not directly ask about taxable income, and instead asks only about ownership and control. Any authority the IRS has to ask the foreign bank question is derived from the Bank Secrecy Act, which requires US persons to file a Report of Foreign Bank and Financial Accounts (FBAR) if they have:

1)   financial interest in, signature authority or other authority over one or more accounts, such as bank accounts, brokerage accounts and mutual funds, in a foreign country; and

2)   the aggregate value of all foreign financial accounts exceeds $10,000 at any time during the calendar year.

Taxpayers required to complete the FBAR generally must report their foreign financial accounts on a Form 8938, and file the form along with their Form 1040.

In the US, taxpayers are legally required to give the IRS enough information to calculate their taxes. However, if a taxpayer reports all crypto transactions, it is difficult to discern a legitimate reason for the crypto question, other than putting taxpayers on notice that the IRS is watching, and subjecting taxpayers to penalties if they answer incorrectly.

From the IRS perspective, a likely rationale for the IRS inclusion of the crypto question may be found in an October 2019 keynote speech at the Brookings Institute by IRS Chief Counsel Michael Desmond entitled *Cryptocurrency and Tax Administration*. In that speech, Desmond noted that an estimated eight percent of US adults hold some form of crypto, and based on that, the IRS should receive roughly 12 million returns reporting crypto transactions. However, he stated the IRS received "nowhere near that" amount, and "we [the IRS] think there's a high degree of non-compliance."

A related IRS disclosure issue is whether holders of crypto on foreign exchanges are also required to report their holdings on Form 8938. Under current law, it is unclear whether an account on a foreign crypto exchange would be considered an account at a foreign financial institution. In section 1471(d)(5), the Code defines a foreign financial institution as:

> *an entity that (a) accepts deposits in the ordinary course of a banking or a similar business, (b) as a substantial portion of its business, holds "financial assets" for the account of the others, or (c) is engaged (or holds itself out as being engaged) primarily in the business of investing, reinvesting or trading in securities, partnership interests, commodities or any interests in such securities, partnership interests or commodities.*

The IRS has not indicated whether it considers foreign crypto exchanges as foreign financial institutions. If it decides to do so, US taxpayers would be required to disclose all such foreign accounts to the IRS, regardless of whether any taxes were due.

The issues with requiring citizens to report their crypto holdings on both the Schedule 1 and the Form 8938 revolve around privacy.

While it is certainly clear the IRS can require citizens to report any gains from crypto, and can require third-party intermediaries to report such gains to both the IRS and the taxpayers, there is no general right for the government to force citizens to disclose mere ownership of any legal assets, be they guns, gold, or crypto. However, by including questions about crypto ownership on tax forms, the IRS seemingly forces US citizens to disclose private financial information to the government, ignoring citizens' rights to keep such information private.

The privacy and constitutional issues related to the crypto question, and the implications for refusing to answer, are troubling. Legally, it is unclear under what authority the IRS can compel an answer to the crypto question. As noted by Chief Justice Roberts in *Rumsfeld v. Forum for Academic and Institutional Rights*:

> *"Some of this Court's leading First Amendment precedents have established the principle that freedom of speech prohibits the government from telling people what they must say."*[69]

Moreover, absent demonstrating to a court a compelling need for the information, the government cannot generally force individuals to disclose certain private information, like whether they own any crypto.[70]

---

[69]   547 U.S. 47 (2006).
[70]   *Whalen v. Roe*, 429 U.S. 589 (1977).

Congressional Action

In March 2020, a bill was introduced in Congress called the Crypto-Currency Act of 2020, which sought to clarify which federal agencies should regulate cryptocurrencies. The bill created a three-part taxonomy of regulation:

1) crypto-commodities regulated by the CFTC,

2) crypto-currencies regulated by FinCEN, and

3) crypto-securities regulated by the SEC.

The Crypto-Currency Act is the second attempt at providing congressional clarity, following the Token Taxonomy Acts of 2018 and 2019, neither of which were passed. The Token Taxonomy Acts would have (i) excluded crypto from the securities laws, and (ii) directed the SEC to:

> *"enact certain regulatory changes regarding digital units secured through public key cryptography, to adjust taxation of virtual currencies held in individual retirement accounts, to create a tax exemption for exchanges of one virtual currency for an-other, to create a de minimis exemption from taxation for gains realized from the sale or exchange of virtual currency for other than cash, and for other purposes."*

The 2019 Token Taxonomy Act was similar in most respects to the 2018 Act, but added a provision that would allow it to supersede state laws in states where laws or regulations overlapped or conflicted with the Act. That provision was likely aimed at New York's much-criticized BitLicense regime. However, that provision would also supersede the more well-received state laws, such as those of Wyoming.

The 2018 Token Taxonomy Act was originally sponsored by Rep. Warren Davidson (R-OH), with five co-sponsors, including three democrats and two republicans. Rep. Davidson is a member of the Congressional Blockchain Caucus, which, as of April 2020, had at least 20 members from both sides of the aisle. According to their website, they are:

> *"a bi-partisan group of Members of Congress and Staff who believe in the future of blockchain technology, and understand that Congress has a role to play in its development. As a Caucus, we have decided on a hands-off regulatory approach, believing that this technology will best evolve the same way the internet did; on its own."* [71]

The Caucus often speaks out on blockchain and crypto issues.

Another bill offered by Rep. Patrick McHenry (R-NC) offers a different approach to crypto regulation. Instead of seeking to pass top-down laws setting forth rules for crypto, Rep. McHenry's bill, called the Financial Services Innovation Act (H.R. 4767), would mandate that federal regulators create Financial Services Innovation Offices (FSIOs) within their agencies. [72] Those FSIOs would create what McHenry describes as a "permanent beta testing" opportunity for companies, similar to regulatory sandbox approach taken by the UK's Financial Conduct Authority. According to McHenry, the Act would allow companies:

> *to provide innovative products or services under an alternative compliance plan, which would provide waivers or modifications to current regulations that are out of date or unduly burdensome. And I think this is a necessary step towards creating a regulatory process that works with financial innovation rather than against it.* [73]

---

[71]   See https://congressionalblockchaincaucus-schweikert.house.gov/about.

[72]   Rep. McHenry first introduced the Financial Services Innovation Act in 2016.

[73]   Congressman Patrick McHenry, *Bitcoin Will Be of Enormous Value,* Unchained Podcast (Oct. 22, 2019).

McHenry has stated the legislation is necessary because the "CFTC and the SEC, as well as the Treasury and the IRS, need to promise some certainty to incentivize entrepreneurs to keep coming up with interesting innovative ideas."[74]

> *Life without knowledge is death in disguise.*
> —Talib Kweli, *K.O.S.*

---

[74] Rehan Yousaf, *US Congressman Patrick McHenry Wants "Yes" Legislation for Crypto and Blockchain*, All-stocks.net (Oct. 24, 2019).